Rhymes, Writing, and Role-Play:

Quick and Easy Lessons for Beginning Readers

Mary A. Lombardo

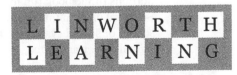

LINWORTH LEARNING

From the Minds of Teachers.

Library of Congress Cataloging-in-Publication Data

Lombardo, Mary A.
  Rhymes, writing, and role-play : quick and easy lessons for beginning
readers / by Mary A. Lombardo.
      p. cm.
  ISBN 1-58683-157-7 (pbk.)
  1. Language arts (Early childhood) 2. Reading (Early childhood) 3.
Nursery rhymes--Study and teaching (Early childhood) 4. Early childhood
education--Activity programs. I. Title.
LB1139.5.L35L66 2004
372.6--dc22

                              2003024776

Published by Linworth Publishing, Inc.
480 East Wilson Bridge Road, Suite L
Worthington, Ohio 43085

ISBN: 1-58683-157-7

5 4 3 2 1

Table of Contents

Table of Contents continued

Overview

Rhyming, Writing and Role-Play: Quick and Easy Lessons for Beginning Readers leads young children through the most important skills for learning to read in a fun and interactive way. They listen to, act out, and recite favorite nursery rhymes, learning about rhyming words and absorbing the rhythm of the English language. They build a sight vocabulary using the list of most commonly used words in the English language. They learn and practice phonic skills based on phonemic awareness and matching letter sounds to letter symbols. They play guessing games that stress comprehension in four interactive plays. Whole language extension activities and student handouts included after each play give rise to creative thinking exercises.

The students enjoy using a readers' theater format to act out short plays, easily reading the simple vocabulary that they have practiced during the oral activities. The student handouts that accompany each play reinforce their developing skills and understandings.

About the Author

Mary Lombardo is a retired teacher who has taught all grade levels from one through six as well as Title 1 reading to at-risk students. For several years she worked in an alternative public school program for home-schooled students, providing curriculum and teaching assistance to parents and half-day instruction to students. She also served as a teacher trainer for the Albuquerque Public Schools.

Teacher Introduction

ORGANIZATION OF THE BOOK

There are four sections in this book, each consisting of two to four chapters.

Section One is all about nursery rhymes. **Chapter One** is an introduction to teaching with the rhymes. **Chapter Two** retells age-old nursery rhymes, providing activities and a student handout for each rhyme. **Chapter Three** lists the most common word families for beginning readers, outlines activities and games to help in making new words, and includes a sample worksheet that can be used as a model for additional handouts. **Chapter Four** is filled with ideas for prompting students to engage in meaningful writing activities.

Section Two focuses on helping students develop a sight word vocabulary and tells where to find a list of the most commonly used words in the English language. **Chapter Five** suggests activities and games that will help students learn these words by sight.

In **Section Three**, each of **Chapters Six** through **Nine** is an interactive play that uses basic vocabulary common to most beginning reading texts. Each play includes activities for decoding practice and problem-solving, whole language extension activities, and a student handout.

In **Section Four,** each of **Chapters Ten** through **Thirteen** is a short play that uses the vocabulary practiced in the interactive plays from the previous chapters. Student handouts are included. **Chapter Fourteen** gives suggestions for additional ways to use role-play as an instructional tool.

OBJECTIVES

1 Help children become aware of like and unlike sounds and match letter symbols to specific sounds.

Children have to be taught to listen for like and unlike sounds. Once they are trained in phonemic awareness, they are ready to match letter symbols to specific sounds.

2 Provide the opportunity to practice basic sight words in an enjoyable venue.

When children are enjoying an activity, they are often unaware that they are learning or practicing learned material. In the interactive plays, the students read sight words to see if they can stump the rest of the class.

3 Develop critical thinking skills.

Critical thinking can be defined as listening to and analyzing information and coming to a sensible conclusion. In the interactive plays, the class members must base their answers to questions posed by the teacher on analyzing the statements from the five actors in the play.

4 Practice phonic skills.
The children use beginning sounds to locate specific words in a series of unfamiliar words.

5 Experience oral reading and performing before an audience.

The actors in each play must read their parts clearly and with suitable expression so their audience can understand them.

6 Develop an ear for rhymes and the rhythm of the English language.

As children participate in learning and repeating nursery rhymes, they develop a sense of the inflections and rhythms of our language and learn how rhymes work—essential steps in learning to read.

7 Practice making words in families, using phonic and rhyming knowledge.

This activity sharpens phonic skills, builds sight vocabulary, and helps children learn one strategy for unlocking new words when they occur.

8 Make meaningful connections between the printed word and the student's experiences.

Comprehending the meaning that printed words convey is one of the most important functions of reading. Making a connection between what is being read and what the child has experienced furthers comprehension.

CORRELATION WITH NCTE STANDARDS

The National Council of Teachers of English (NCTE) has developed 12 standards citing how students should be helped to develop appropriate language skills. The complete list of standards can be found at <www.ncte.com>. The exercises and activities in *Rhymes, Writing, and Role-Play* help students develop the ability to decipher and interpret the written word in a variety of contexts, and to communicate their thoughts and ideas to others. Using the lessons, student handouts, and extended activity suggestions in *Rhymes, Writing and Role-Play*, teachers can easily incorporate the NCTE standards into their curriculum.

How to Use This Book

1 **Read nursery rhymes to the students until they are familiar with them and can recite all or part of them with you.** Do not limit yourself to the rhymes presented here. Nursery rhymes help young children experience the rhythm of our language and develop an ear for rhyming words—two skills that support learning to read.

2 **Write each of the nursery rhymes presented in this book on large wall charts.** As you say the rhymes together, point to the words you are reading. Beginning readers do not realize at first that a set of letters makes a word. By pointing to the words as they are read, children grasp the idea of letters making up words.

3 **Follow the suggestions for games and other activities presented in Chapter One.** These games and activities give children the opportunity to develop many useful skills. They will learn to recognize rhyming words, match words that look similar, recognize beginning sounds, identify the letters that make those sounds, and use letter sounds to make new words.

4 **Work through the activities given in Chapter Two for each nursery rhyme.** Then copy and distribute the student handout and complete it together. Send each handout home with the students along with a short note asking parents to review the handouts with their child. A sample letter is included in **Chapter One**.

5 **Copy the nursery rhyme pages, and ask the students to illustrate them.** Collect the completed pages until all the rhymes have been reviewed, and put together a book of the rhymes for each child.

6 **Do the suggested activities for learning about common word families given in Chapter Three.** Then work on developing the students' writing skills by adding the ideas in **Chapter Four** to your own favorite writing activities.

7 **When you are working with your students to build a sight vocabulary, practice the vocabulary from the first interactive play in Chapter Seven.** These words are *I*, *will*, *go*, *with*, *you*, *no*, *yes*, *to*, *the*, *store*, *not*. See **Section Two** for information on where to find the list of most commonly used words in the English language along with suggestions for teaching those words.

8 **Get ready to perform in interactive plays.** When students have completed the activities and handouts from **Section One** and learned the sight words from the first interactive play, *I Do Not Like It*, explain to them that they will be playing some guessing games. Five students will be reading to the class, and the rest of the students will see if they can guess which student does or does not like certain things. Perform the four interactive plays as many times as the students wish, and complete the accompanying handouts.

9 **Read each short play in Section Four to the students, and ask them to predict the ending before reading the plays together as a class.** After the children have read all the plays and completed the handouts, divide the class into small groups, and assign a play to each group. Each play gives the number of students needed in the cast. These plays can be presented within the classroom or to other classes.

Nursery Rhymes: A Playful Introduction to Reading

Hearing and learning nursery rhymes can be one of the best experiences children can have to start them off on the right road to reading.

1 They are fun, so children enjoy hearing, reciting, or singing them.

2 They present concrete pictures that help children derive meaning from the written word. Children can easily visualize and make a connection with Mary's pet following along behind her, or Jack tumbling down a hill and hurting his head.

3 They present a way to build vocabulary. What is a tuffet? *(a low seat)* What are curds and whey? *(cottage cheese)* Have you ever eaten a plum? What is a stack of hay, and what is it used for?

4 The familiar key words from the rhymes can be used to teach beginning sounds.

5 The familiar words from the rhymes can also be used to build word families, such as *miss, kiss, hiss; Jack, back, pack, rack; Jill, bill, fill, hill; and boy, joy, toy.*

6 Answering questions about the rhymes fosters critical thinking skills and provides writing practice.

Seven nursery rhymes are presented in this section along with suggestions for using them to introduce reading skills and understandings to students. Each rhyme is followed by two student handouts: one addresses skills learned, and one is a copy of the rhyme that the children can illustrate and compile to make their own nursery rhyme books.

Chapter One
INTRODUCING THE RHYMES

The first step in introducing the rhymes to your students is simply to read and enjoy them. You might want to begin or end the school day with a few rhymes or read some every day before you read a story to the class. It will not take long for the students to begin to remember the lines, and you should encourage them to chime in when they do.

Seven rhymes are included here, but there are books of nursery rhymes that include many other enjoyable familiar and unfamiliar ones. The Internet is another good source for finding additional nursery rhymes. If you go to <www.google.com> and enter "nursery rhymes," you will find many useful sites. At <www.enchantedlearning.com> you will find lessons for teaching the nursery rhymes as well as pages you can print for nursery rhyme coloring books and calendars.

To use the reading/writing handouts provided in this book most effectively, complete them as a class, and then send them home to be shared with parents. A good way to make sure the papers are reviewed at home is to initiate a system of rewards. This can be as simple as a gold star every time a handout is brought back to school signed by a parent as proof that the child has read it at home. This book provides a sample letter to parents asking them to do this.

The reading/writing handouts include three tasks: making words from words in the rhymes, using the words by filling in the blanks in a sentence, and writing short answers to questions. In the first few handouts, the children will be asked to write yes and no answers to questions, and in later ones, to respond in short sentences. Also, choosing and circling the name of the day of the week on each handout gives the teacher an opportunity for a short beginning sound lesson.

Shown here is a sample letter you can copy to send home asking parents to share in their child's learning adventures by reviewing the student handouts at home and returning them to you at school.

Sample Letter to Parents

Date:

Dear Parent:

As your child enters the exciting world of reading, we would like to work with you to make this experience a rewarding and happy one.

Your child will be bringing home worksheets that we have completed together at school. Please read over the worksheets with your child, sign them to show they have been reviewed, and send them back to me at school.

Each time a worksheet is brought back to school, your child will be recognized to show he or she is growing as a good reader.

Thank you for your help.

Sincerely,

★ ★ ✔ General Activities ★ ★

✔ LEARNING THE RHYMES

Print the rhyme on a large piece of chart paper. If possible, use pictures to represent some of the words. For example, in "Mary Had a Little Lamb," you could use a curly lamb, a small schoolhouse, and stick figure children.

Point out the pictures and words within the rhyme. Ask students to identify the pictures, then read the rhyme along with you. Point to the words as you read them.

Ask two types of questions about the rhyme: questions that can be answered by what the children have heard and questions that promote critical thinking. For example, in "Wee Willie Winkie," your questions might be:

What is he wearing?

What is he doing?

Is he a grownup or a child? Is he big or small?

Why does he want all the children in bed?

Do you think it is summer or winter? What made you think this?

To stimulate comprehension, act out the rhyme. This can be an enjoyable activity, as children usually love dramatic play. In "Jack and Jill," for instance, two children can walk along pretending they are going uphill and then fall, one after the other.

Make simple bag or stick puppets to represent the characters in the rhyme. Divide the class into groups, and assign a different nursery rhyme to each group.

Point out that words form sentences and make sense in a certain order. Choose one or several lines from the rhyme, and write the words on pieces of cardboard or construction paper. Distribute the words to the students, and ask them to line up in the order that the line is read.

Split lines from several of the rhymes in half, and write each half sentence on a different index card. Distribute the cards. Children must find the part of the sentence that completes the one they are holding, for example, one card might read *Jack and Jill,* while another card reads *went up the hill.*

✔ RHYMING

Read two or more, if needed, lines from the rhyme, emphasizing the rhyming words. Ask the children to listen for the words that sound alike.

List the words that rhyme and are spelled alike on the board. Ask the students to put a line under the letters that are alike in each of the words. For instance, day and play from "Mary Had a Little Lamb," Jill and hill from "Jack and Jill," and horn and corn from "Little Boy Blue."

Make up short rhymes and ask the students to fill in the missing word orally. Here are some examples:

1 Did you ever see a cat / with a great big h—? (hat)
You make the "h" sound and gesture as if you are putting on a hat. The children fill in the word *hat*.

2 I saw a spotted bug / crawling on my r—. (rug)

3 In my rocket very soon / I will go flying to the m—. (moon)

4 I can drive very far / in my father's great big c—. (car)

5 I like to look / at a pretty picture b—. (book)

Other rhyming partners are *fun, sun; late, gate; bunny, funny; wish, dish;* and *bake, cake*.
Borrow others from the nursery rhymes.

✔ BEGINNING SOUNDS

The first step in letter sound recognition is developing an ear for like and unlike sounds: phonemic awareness. This is best accomplished by saying words that begin and do not begin alike and asking students to tell you whether the words start the same. Point to objects around the room or show pictures from magazines or books, say the names of the objects, and ask if the words start the same. Do this activity as often as you can before putting letter symbols together with letter sounds.

Use teamwork to learn letter names and sounds. Your students may already have learned many of their letters and beginning sounds in kindergarten, but it is important to review them. Post the alphabet in the room, and ask children to point to letters you name as well as letters that begin words you give them. Make a game of this by placing students in teams. The team members can help each other find the correct letters. All the teams can be winners, as there can be a first winner, a second winner, and so on.

Choose words from the rhymes to review, or teach specific beginning sounds. Some rhymes lend themselves to this readily, but words can be found in any of the rhymes for this purpose. It's easy to see that "Wee Willie Winkie" is perfect for teaching the sound of **w** and "Jack and Jill" for the **j** sound, but any word from any rhyme can be used to teach an effective lesson.

Point to pictures in magazines or objects around the classroom that begin with the letters you are teaching, and say their names, emphasizing the beginning sound. Be creative. A picture of a salad can be lettuce; a woman can be mother. Ask the students to find pictures or objects that begin with sounds they have learned.

Post some pictures that begin with the letters you are teaching. These can be cut from magazines or coloring books. Say the names of the pictures, emphasizing the beginning sounds. Then ask the student to tell you which ones match.

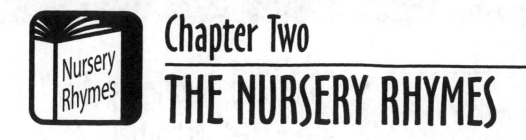

Chapter Two
THE NURSERY RHYMES

There are seven nursery rhymes in this chapter:

1 "One, Two, Buckle My Shoe"

Beginning sounds for **d** and **s**

2 "Mary Had a Little Lamb"

Beginning sounds for **g, m,** and **l**

3 "Little Jack Horner"

Beginning sounds for **p, c,** and **j**

4 "Little Boy Blue"

Beginning sounds for **b** and **h**

5 "Humpty Dumpty"

Beginning sounds for **k, f,** and **t**

6 "Wee Willie Winkie"

Beginning sounds for **w, r,** and **n**

7 "Jack and Jill"

Beginning sound for **v** and a review of all sounds

1. "One, Two, Buckle My Shoe"

One, two,

Buckle my shoe.

Three, four,

Shut the door.

Five, six,

Pick up sticks.

Seven, eight,

Lay them straight.

Nine, ten,

A big, red hen.

"One, Two, Buckle My Shoe"
★ ★ ✔ Activities ★ ★

1 Read the rhyme several times. Assign pairs of students to read or recite each stanza, standing as they say their two lines, then sitting as the next two lines are said by other students.

2 Practice the beginning sound **d**: *door, dog, doll, desk, deck, don't, dime, dozen, diamond.* Read the list of words beginning with **d** several times. Then write a **d** on the board explaining that the words begin with the letter **d.** Read the list again, inserting words that begin with a different letter, for example, *door, dog, happy, doll, mother,* and so on. Ask the children to clap or stand to indicate when they hear a word beginning with **d.**

3 Practice the beginning sound **s**: *six, Sam, socks, silly, sat, sore, sand, seesaw, soccer.* Follow the directions for the letter **d.**

4 Write the number pairs on the board: *1, 2   3, 4   5, 6   7, 8   9, 10* Present the following rhymes in the correct order without saying the number words, and ask the children which numbers they match.

Set One
Give me the glue (one, two)
Give me some more (three, four)
I have something to fix (five, six)
It's a broken gate (seven, eight)
It's fixed again (nine, ten)

Set Two
A ghost said "Boo" (one, two)
He knocked at the door (three, four)
He did some tricks (five, six)
It was very late (seven, eight)
He ran away then (nine, ten)

Then try some rhymes out of order:
I swim at the shore (three, four)
A cow says moo (one, two)
I cannot wait (seven, eight)
Forty-one kicks (five, six)
A bear in his den (nine, ten)

Some students may be able to think of words that rhyme and fit into the poem. Encourage them to do so.

5 Write all the sets of rhymes on chart paper or on the board. While half the class reads a rhyme with you, the others in the class can pantomime the words as they are read.

6 Write the number words on the board, and ask the students if they can write the correct number after each word. Have a chart that has the words and matching numbers nearby for easy referral.

7 Writing practice: Write the number words one through ten with the correct numbers after them.

8 Connections: Ask the children to tell how they fasten their shoes. Is it with a buckle, shoelaces, Velcro, zippers? Write those words on the board, and ask the children to write their name below the word that describes how they fasten their shoes.

9 Connections: Ask if any of the children have played the game "pick up sticks." These games are inexpensive, and it would be fun to show them how to play.

10 Distribute the copy of the rhyme for the children to illustrate, Student Handout #1. Collect the pictures and hold to incorporate into individual nursery rhyme books.

11 Distribute Student Handout #2, and complete together. Send home for reading homework practice.

"One, Two, Buckle My Shoe" Student Handout #1

My name is _____ .

One, Two, Buckle My Shoe

One, two,
Buckle my shoe.
Three, four,
Shut the door.
Five, six,
Pick up sticks.
Seven, eight,
Lay them straight.
Nine, ten,
A big, red hen.

Draw a picture about something from this rhyme.

"One, Two, Buckle My Shoe" Student Handout #2

My name is _____.

Today is Monday   Tuesday   Wednesday   Thursday   Friday.

Let's make words.

Thr<u>ee</u>   s ____ ____   f<u>ive</u>   d ____ ____ ____

<u>pick</u>   s ____ ____ ____   l<u>ay</u>   s ____ ____

<u>ten</u>   d ____ ____   n<u>ine</u>   d ____ ____ ____

Let's use our words.

I _____ in a pool.   five   dive

I will _____ a toy.   pick   sick

Here are _____ dogs.   three   me

Let's write. Write yes or no.

Do you have a dog?_____

Do you feel sick?_____

Do you have ten toes?_____

Write dogs or cats. Do you like dogs or cats best? _____

2. "Mary Had a Little Lamb"

Mary had a little lamb

Its fleece was white as snow

And everywhere that Mary went

The lamb was sure to go.

It followed her to school one day.

That was against the rule.

It made the children laugh and play

To see a lamb in school.

"Mary Had a Little Lamb"
★ ★ ✔ Activities ★ ★

1 Read the rhyme several times, encouraging students to join in when they know the words. Write the rhyme on a large piece of chart paper, and read it aloud with the students. Use pictures for some of the words if you like.

2 Practice the beginning sound **m:** *Mary, mother, mom, mad, me, mine, monkey, mitten.* Read the list of words several times. Write an **m** on the board, and explain that the words begin with the letter **m**. Read the list again, inserting words that begin with different letters: *Mary, mother, baby, mom, store,* and so on. Ask the children to clap or stand when they hear a word beginning with **m**.

3 Practice the beginning sound **l:** *laugh, lamb, lollipop, love, little, lemon, lost, look* and the beginning sound **g:** *go, get, gone, give, gave, game, got, goose, geese, gum.* Follow the directions given for the letter **m**.

4 Play "Follow the Leader" by having one person pretend to be Mary with the rest of the class pretending to be lambs. They follow wherever she goes.

5 Discuss why the children laughed at Mary's lamb at school. Ask the children to draw another animal that would make them laugh if it came to school.

6 Writing Practice: Write the words *This is a* on the board, and ask the children to copy them under the picture they drew (in #5). Have them try to add the name of the animal they have drawn by listening to the letters in the word. Some children may hear and write only one letter; others may hear and write several of the letters. Praise them all!

7 Connections: Have the children relate stories about pets they have or would like to have. Did their pets ever do anything that made someone laugh? What did their pet do?

8 Distribute the copy of the rhyme for the children to illustrate, Student Handout #1. Collect the pictures and hold to incorporate into individual nursery rhyme books.

9 Distribute Student Handout #2, and complete together. Send home for reading homework practice.

"Mary Had a Little Lamb" Student Handout #1

My name is _____.

Mary Had a Little Lamb

Mary had a little lamb
Its fleece was white as snow
And everywhere that Mary went
The lamb was sure to go.
It followed her to school one day.
That was against the rule.
It made the children laugh and play
To see a lamb in school.

Draw a picture about Mary and her lamb.

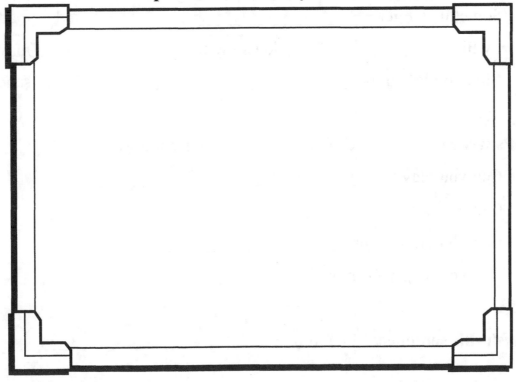

"Mary Had a Little Lamb" Student Handout #2

My name is _____.

Today is Monday   Tuesday   Wednesday   Thursday   Friday.

Let's make words.

had   d ___ ___   m ___ ___   s ___ ___   l ___ ___

play   d ___ ___   l ___ ___   m ___ ___   s ___ ___

and   l ___ ___ ___   s ___ ___ ___

set   g ___ ___   l ___ ___

Let's use our words.

Sometimes I get _____.   lad   mad

I will _____ down my toy.   lay   may

I like to play in the _____.   land   sand

Let's write.   **Yes I can.**   **No I cannot.**

Can you play?_____

Can you eat? _____

Can you drive a car? _____

Can you help your mom? _____

Finish this sentence. I like to _____.

3. "Little Jack Horner"

Little Jack Horner
Sat in the corner
Eating his Christmas pie.
He put in his thumb
And pulled out a plum
And said what a good boy am I!

"Little Jack Horner"
★ ★ ☑ Activities ★ ★

1 Read the rhyme several times until the children can say it along with you.

2 Practice the beginning sound **c:** *came, can, come, cat, car, call, corner, cook, cool, coop.* Read the list of words beginning with **c** several times. Write a **c** on the board, and explain that this is the letter that makes the **c** sound. Then read the list again, inserting words that begin with a different letter, for example, *came, can, door, big, come, see, cat, car, mother, call, boy,* and so on. Ask the children to clap or stand to indicate when they hear a word beginning with the letter **c.**

3 Practice the beginning sound **p:** *pat, puppy, pencil, part, pig, penny, pin, pack, pew.* Follow the directions for the letter **c.**

4 Practice the beginning sound **j:** *jar, junk, jump, jelly, jam, jungle, just, Jeffrey, jiffy.* Follow the directions for the letter **c.**

5 Have the children trace around their two hands on a large piece of paper. Label the left hand and the right hand. Then count the number of thumbs, and below their tracing, write the sentence *I have two thumbs.*

6 Look through magazines to find pictures of various fruits. Paste them on a large sheet of chart paper, and label them. Underline the beginning letter of each word that begins with a consonant, and review them with the students.

7 Connections: Discuss the reason some children may have to sit in a corner. Ask for examples of the misbehavior that could put someone in timeout in a corner or in their room. Ask why they think Jack Horner was sitting in a corner. What might he have done? Does he think he deserves to be in the corner? *(He thinks he's a good boy.)*

8 Connections: Ask students: What is a Christmas pie? What special holiday foods do you eat?

9 Distribute the copy of the rhyme for the children to illustrate, Student Handout #1. Collect the pictures and hold to incorporate into individual nursery rhyme books.

10 Distribute Student Handout #2, and complete together. Send home for reading homework practice.

"Little Jack Horner" Student Handout #1

My name is _____.

Little Jack Horner

Little Jack Horner
Sat in the corner
Eating his Christmas pie.
He put in his thumb
And pulled out a plum
And said what a good boy am I!

Draw a picture about Jack Horner.

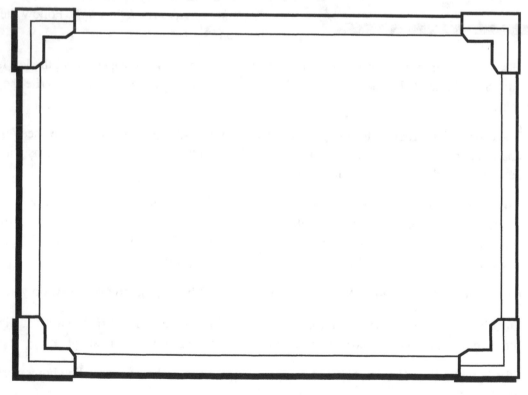

"Little Jack Horner" Student Handout #2

My name is _____.

Today is Monday   Tuesday   Wednesday   Thursday   Friday.

Let's make words.

J<u>ack</u>	l ___ ___ ___	p ___ ___ ___	s ___ ___ ___
s<u>at</u>	p ___ ___	c ___ ___	m ___ ___
<u>in</u>	d ___ ___	p ___ ___	
th<u>umb</u>	d ___ ___ ___	cr ___ ___ ___	
st<u>uck</u>	d ___ ___ ___	l ___ ___ ___	s ___ ___ ___
	m ___ ___ ___		

Let's use our words.

Jack is _____ the car.   pin   in

He _____ on a tack.   sat   mat

I can _____ .   may   play

Let's write. It is funny. It is not funny.

Jack sat on a hat. _____.

Jack sat on a tack. _____.

Jack sat in a chair. _____.

Finish this sentence. I like to eat _____.

4. "Little Boy Blue"

Little Boy Blue
Come blow your horn.
The cow's in the meadow,
The sheep's in the corn.
Where is the little boy
Who cares for the sheep?
He's under the haystack
Fast asleep.

"Little Boy Blue"
★ ★ ✔ Activities ★ ★

1 Read the rhyme with the children, and encourage them to say the words with you.

2 Practice the beginning sound **b**: *bat, back, bake, beet, Bill, boy, boat, bike, buy.* Read the list of words beginning with **b** several times Write a **b** on the board, and explain that the words begin with the letter **b.** Then read the list again, inserting words that begin with a different letter, for example, *bat, back, happy, dog, mother, beet, Bill,* and so on. Ask the children to clap or stand to indicate when they hear a word beginning with **b.**

3 Practice the beginning sound **h**: *horn, happy, high, hop, hope, hill, heavy, hay, hunt.* Follow the directions for the letter **b.**

4 Write each of the words *red, yellow,* and *blue* on separate sheets of chart paper. Give the children magazines and scissors, and tell them they have a specified amount of time to look through the magazines to find and cut out any objects that are those three colors. Have them use beginning sounds to help decide on which of the three charts the pictures belong. Ask them to tape their pictures to the appropriate chart. Label the pictures.

5 Read the rhyme. Discuss what a haystack is and what color it would be *(yellow),* what the little boy is probably wearing *(blue jeans if he is working on a farm),* and other colors you might find on a farm *(red barn, white fence, blue sky, green grass, and plants).*

6 Write the words *red, yellow, blue, white,* and *green* on the board. Tell the children you will be asking them to go to the board and point to the correct color of words you will tell them. Say words such as *clouds, sky, jeans, grass, a dollar bill, lamb, star, sun, lips, a rose, a ghost, eyes (blue* or *green),* and so on.

7 Writing Practice: Show the students how to fold a piece of drawing paper in half twice, ending up with four boxes, and have them do this. Tell them they will be writing four sentences, one in each box, and drawing pictures to go with their words. Each sentence will begin with *This is a.* Write these three words on the board. They will write a color word and choose a fifth word to complete the sentence. They will spell the last word by listening to the letters they hear and then illustrate the sentence. Demonstrate by writing *This is a red ball.* Show how you can write the word *ball* by listening to the letters. For example, ask: What do I hear at the beginning of the word ball? and What other letters do I hear? Help with spelling the words.

8 Reread the rhyme, encouraging the children to chime in when they remember the words. Ask the following questions:

> *Where is the little boy?*
> *What is he doing?*
> *Why did he lay down on the pile of hay?*
> *What is the little boy's job?*
> *How will the farmer feel when he sees the little boy is not doing his job?*

9 Connections: Ask the students to talk about jobs or chores they are given at home. If they did not do their jobs, how would their parents feel? What would they do?

10 Distribute the copy of the rhyme for the children to illustrate, Student Handout #1. Collect the pictures and hold to incorporate into individual nursery rhyme books.

11 Distribute Student Handout #2, and complete together. Send home for reading homework practice.

"Little Boy Blue"
Student Handout #1

My name is _____.

Little Boy Blue

Little Boy Blue
Come blow your horn.
The cow's in the meadow,
The sheep's in the corn.
Where is the little boy
Who cares for the sheep?
He's under the haystack
Fast asleep.

Draw a picture about Little Boy Blue.

"Little Boy Blue"
Student Handout #2

My name is _____.

Today is Monday   Tuesday   Wednesday   Thursday   Friday.

Let's make words.

b<u>oy</u>   j ___ ___   t ___ ___

c<u>ow</u>   b ___ ___   h ___ ___   p ___ ___

c<u>orn</u>   b ___ ___ ___   h ___ ___ ___

h<u>ay</u>   d ___ ___   l ___ ___   m ___ ___

Let's use our words.

I can blow a _____.   corn   horn

I have a new _____.   joy   toy

I will ask mom if I _____go.   may   day

Let's write. Fill in the words.

Little _____ Blue / Come blow your horn.   Boy   Toy

The _____ in the meadow,   cow's   now's

The sheep's in the _____.   corn   horn

Where is the little _____   toy   boy

Who cares for the sheep?

He's under the haystack _____ asleep.   fast   last

5. "Humpty Dumpty"

Humpty Dumpty sat on a wall.

Humpty Dumpty had a great fall.

All the king's horses

And all the King's men

Couldn't put Humpty together again.

"Humpty Dumpty"
★ ★ ✓ Activities ★ ★

1. Read the rhyme a few times. This is a simple rhyme to learn, and the children should be chanting it with you in no time.

2. Act it out. One student pretends to fall from a wall. The king's men gallop up, and all try to put Humpty together.

3. Practice the beginning sound **k:** *king, kingdom, kitchen, key, karate, kayak, keep, kazoo.* Read the list of words beginning with **k** several times. Write a **k** on the board, and explain that the words begin with the letter **k.** Read the list again, inserting words that begin with a different letter, for example, *king, kingdom, help, kitchen, sigh, key, happy, dog, mother, karate,* and so on. Ask the children to clap or stand to indicate when they hear a word beginning with the letter **k.**

4. Practice the beginning sound **f:** *fat, finger, fill, fight, full, fork, feather, fly, father, fur.* Follow the directions for the letter **k.**

5. Practice the beginning sound **t:** *tan, time, ten, till, take, took, toot, tough, temper, tame, tool.* Follow the directions for the letter **k.**

6. Pair the students, and give each pair a purchased jigsaw puzzle, or one that is made by cutting the front of a cereal box into sections that can be easily fitted together. Students pretend they are the king's men trying to put Humpty together, and they put the puzzle together as quickly as they can.

7. Connections: Hold a class discussion about times when students or people they know have fallen and broken legs, arms, and so on. How were they put together? Who helped them? Could Humpty Dumpty be helped in the same way?

8. Distribute the copy of the rhyme for the children to illustrate, Student Handout #1. Collect the pictures and hold to incorporate into individual nursery rhyme books.

9. Distribute Student Handout #2, and complete together. Send home for reading homework practice.

"Humpty Dumpty" Student Handout #1

My name is _____.

Humpty Dumpty

Humpty Dumpty sat on a wall.

Humpty Dumpty had a great fall.

All the king's horses

And all the King's men

Couldn't put Humpty together again.

Draw a picture about Humpty Dumpty.

"Humpty Dumpty" Student Handout #2

My name is _____.

Today is Monday   Tuesday   Wednesday   Thursday   Friday.

Let's make words.

s<u>at</u>	b ___ ___	f ___ ___	h ___ ___
w<u>all</u>	b ___ ___ ___	f ___ ___ ___	t ___ ___ ___
<u>k</u>ing	s ___ ___ ___	p ___ ___ ___	
m<u>en</u>	h ___ ___ ___	p ___ ___	t ___ ___

Let's use our words.

The cat is _____.   fat   hat

The king can _____.   ping   sing

I am on a _____.   tall   wall

The _____ are at the wall.   ten   men

Let's write.   **Yes, he did.**   **No, he did not.**

Did Humpty Dumpty sit on a wall? _____.

Did Humpty Dumpty fall? _____.

Did he get hurt? _____.

Did he get put together again? _____.

Finish this sentence.

I can sit on _____.

6. "Wee Willie Winkie"

Wee Willie Winkie
Runs through the town,
Upstairs and downstairs
In his night gown,
Rapping at the windows,
Crying through the lock,
"Are the children in their beds,
For now it's eight o'clock."

"Wee Willie Winkie"
★ ★ ✓ Activities ★ ★

1 Discuss the word "rapping," and find as many other words that have the same or almost the same meaning, for example, *knocking, tapping, banging, pounding.* Ask students to demonstrate each of the words they have suggested to show the various shades of meaning.

2 Practice the beginning sound **w:** *want, went, will, wish, weep, walk, whisper, wash.* Read the list of words beginning with **w** several times. Write a **w** on the board, and explain that the words begin with the letter **w.** Then read the list again, inserting words that begin with a different letter, for example, *want, went, have, go, cat, wish, weep, dog, mother, whisper, wash,* and so on. Ask the children to clap or stand to indicate when they hear a word beginning with the letter **w.**

3 Practice the beginning sound **r:** *ran, rabbit, red, rug, rule, rubber, rag, rat, rich, really.* Follow the directions for the letter **w.**

4 Practice the beginning sound **n:** *no, nut, nice, never, nose, nickel, nap, neat, night, niece.* Follow the directions for the letter **w.**

5 Connections: Discuss the fact that Willie is wearing a nightgown. In olden days boys and men wore nightgowns, and small boys wore dresses. How has that changed today? What type of nightwear do people wear today?

6 Connections: Discuss bed times. What time do the children go to bed? Is it at eight o'clock as it is in the rhyme? Can they stay up later on some nights? Have a mini health lesson: talk about the advantages of a good night's sleep. Ask the children to talk about times when they didn't get enough sleep versus times when they did.

7 Distribute the copy of the rhyme for the children to illustrate, Student Handout #1. Collect the pictures and hold to incorporate into individual nursery rhyme books.

8 Distribute Student Handout #2, and complete together. Send home for reading homework practice.

"Wee Willie Winkie" Student Handout #1

My name is _____.

Wee Willie Winkie

Wee Willie Winkie
Runs through the town,
Upstairs and downstairs
In his night gown,
Rapping at the windows,
Crying through the lock,
"Are the children in their beds,
For now it's eight o'clock."

Draw a picture about Wee Willie Winkie.

"Wee Willie Winkie" Student Handout #2

My name is _____.

Today is Monday   Tuesday   Wednesday   Thursday   Friday.

Let's make words.

b<u>ed</u>	r ___ ___	f ___ ___	w ___ ___
<u>lock</u>	s ___ ___ ___	r ___ ___ ___	
t<u>own</u>	br ___ ___ ___	g ___ ___ ___	
<u>and</u>	h ___ ___ ___	s ___ ___ ___	
n<u>ow</u>	b ___ ___	c ___ ___	h ___ ___ ___ w ___ ___

Let's use our words.

The _____ gives us milk.   bow   cow

I live in a _____.   brown   town

I can put on a _____.   rock   sock

I have a _____ hat.   red   bed

Let's write. Fix the mixed up sentences.

cat The brown is _____.

in bed I sleep _____.

see a cow I _____.

Finish this sentence.

I do not like to _____.

7. "Jack and Jill"

Jack and Jill

Went up the hill

To fetch a pail of water.

Jack fell down

And broke his crown

And Jill came tumbling after.

Up Jack got

And home did trot

As fast as he could caper.

Went to bed

To mend his head

With vinegar and brown paper.

"Jack and Jill"
✔ Activities

1 Read the rhyme several times. If you know the tune, teach the children to sing it.

2 Practice the beginning sound **v:** *vinegar, victory, vim, Vaseline, village, villain, very, vacation.* Read the list of words beginning with **v** several times. Write a **v** on the board, and explain that the words begin with the letter **v.** Then read the list again, inserting words that begin with a different letter, for example, *vinegar, victory, want, have, go, vim, Vaseline, cat, wish, dog, mother, village, villain, wash,* and so on. Ask the children to clap or stand when they hear a word beginning with the letter **v.**

3 Use this rhyme for reviewing all the sounds learned to date: **b:** *broke, bed;* **c:** *crown, could, caper, came;* **d:** *down;* **f:** *fast, fetch, fell;* **g:** *got;* **h:** *hill, home, his, head;* **j:** *Jack, Jill;* **m:** *mend;* **p:** *pail, paper;* **t:** *tumbling, trot, to;* **v:** *vinegar;* **w:** *water, went, with.*

4 Discuss the many containers that can hold liquids: *pail, bucket, box, vase, bottle, jar, glass, cup, pot, bowl,* and any others the children suggest. When would each most likely be used? For example, a vase would be used for water for flowers, a glass for something for a person to drink from, and a bowl for cooking or for a pet's drinking water. Why would Jack and Jill take a pail? *(probably because a pail has a handle and is easier to carry)*

5 List several different words that indicate object size, for example, *little, small, wee, tiny, teensy, microscopic, large, big, enormous, gigantic.* Discuss the differences in meaning. Have the students identify objects of each size. Ask what size pail the children were probably carrying. Why does that size pail make sense?

6 Connections: Discuss times when the children have fallen. Ask them to draw a picture of a time when they or someone they know fell, and help them write a sentence about it. Post the pictures on the bulletin board along with the sentences, and read them to the class. If the children can, ask them to read their own sentence and those of others.

7 Connections: Jack and Jill were given a chore to do and did not do a good job. Ask the children to tell about times when they have been given something to do and either did a good job or did not do as good a job as they could have.

8 Write the letters *c g j m s t w* on the board, leaving room under them to write words. Ask the children to tell you what drinks start with those letters. *(Coke, cola, cranberry juice, Gatorade, juice, milk, soda, tea, water)* If they suggest other liquids starting with other letters, add them to the board. Ask the students to choose one beverage and write a sentence or two describing it and telling why they like that one best, for example: *Milk is white. It is good with cookies.*

9 Distribute the copy of the rhyme for the children to illustrate Student Handout #1. Collect the pictures and hold to incorporate into individual nursery rhyme books.

10 Distribute Student Handout #2, and complete together. Send home for reading homework practice.

11 Assemble the nursery rhyme books. Distribute the nursery rhyme pages the children have illustrated, and tell them you are going to put them in the order of the alphabet. Say the alphabet. When you come to a letter that starts one of the rhymes, ask what rhyme begins with that letter. The order will be: "Humpty Dumpty," "Jack and Jill," "Little Boy Blue," "Little Jack Horner," "Mary Had a Little Lamb," "One, Two, Buckle My Shoe," and "Wee Willie Winkie." Have the children number the pages.

12 Give each child a piece of lined paper. Help the children write the names of the rhymes in alphabetical order, one rhyme per line, adding the number of the page. Explain to them that this is the way books are put together so people will know where to find certain things. The children can design covers with their names and a title. Staple the books together, or punch holes and use colored yarn to assemble.

"Jack and Jill" Student Handout #1

My name is _____.

Jack and Jill

Jack and Jill
Went up the hill
To fetch a pail of water.
Jack fell down
And broke his crown
And Jill came tumbling after.
Up Jack got
And home did trot
As fast as he could caper.
Went to bed
To mend his head
With vinegar and brown paper.

Draw a picture about Jack and Jill.

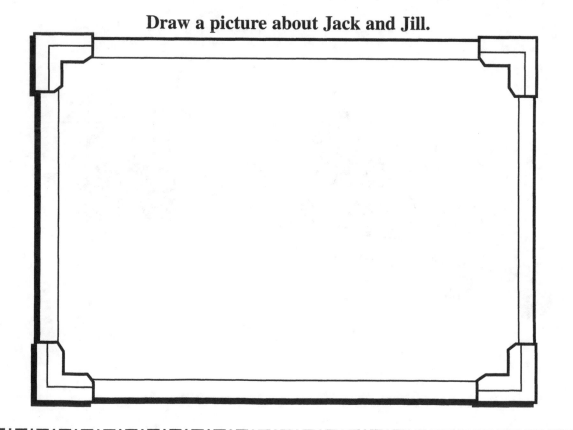

"Jack and Jill" Student Handout #2

My name is _____.

Today is Monday   Tuesday   Wednesday   Thursday   Friday.

Let's make words.

<u>Jack</u>	b ___ ___ ___	p ___ ___ ___	s ___ ___ ___	t ___ ___
<u>Jill</u>	B ___ ___ ___	f ___ ___ ___	h ___ ___ ___	
	p ___ ___ ___	w ___ ___ ___		
<u>down</u>	br ___ ___ ___	cr ___ ___ ___	g ___ ___ ___	t ___ ___ ___
<u>got</u>	c ___ ___	d ___ ___	h ___ ___	l ___ ___
	n ___ ___	p ___ ___	r ___ ___	
<u>fast</u>	c ___ ___ ___	l ___ ___ ___	m ___ ___ ___	
	p ___ ___ ___	v ___ ___ ___		

Let's use our words.

I will _____ my bag.   sack   pack

A king has a gold _____.   town   crown

Mom cooks in a big _____.   pot   not

Let's write. What do you do with a friend?

_____

_____

_____

Chapter Three

WORD FAMILIES

Once your students are on their way to identifying beginning sounds, it's important to see if they can make other words using the sounds they hear. There are hundreds of common endings in the English language. Listed here you will find those that you will most likely use in first and second grade. By making new words orally, you are training students to recognize sounds that are alike and different, even if they are not yet connecting the letter form with the letter sound. This phonemic awareness will lead to putting together sounds with the letters they represent and, ultimately, to extending their reading vocabulary.

Most Common Word Families

ack back Jack lack sack tack
ad bad dad had lad mad pad sad
ail bail fail hail jail mail nail pail rail sail tail wail
ake bake cake fake lake make rake take wake
all ball call fall hall mall tall wall
ame came fame game lame name same tame
an can Dan fan man pan ran tan
and band hand land sand
ap cap lap map nap rap sap tap
at bat cat fat hat mat pat rat sat
ay bay day gay hay jay lay may pay ray say way
eep beep deep jeep keep peep sleep weep
en Ben hen men pen ten when
ent bent dent lent rent sent tent went
ide hide ride side tide wide
ight fright light might night right sight tight
in bin fin kin pin sin tin win
ing king ring sing wing
it bit fit hit kit lit pit sit
oat boat coat float goat
ump bump dump jump lump pump

Word Families
★ ★ ✔ Activities ★ ★

1 **Use the familiar words of the nursery rhymes as an introduction to word families.** List the words and point out the letters in each word that are the same. See if the students can read the words with you using the rhyming ending and the beginning sounds they have learned.

Mary Had a Little Lamb

white	went	go	day
bite	bent	no	hay
kite	dent	so	may
site	sent	ho	say

Little Jack Horner

sat	thumb	boy	am
cat	numb	toy	bam
fat	dumb	joy	clam
bat	crumb	Roy	ham

Little Boy Blue

blow	horn	cow	sheep
grow	born	how	sleep
crow	corn	now	weep
low	torn	plow	deep

Wee Willie Winkie

wee	Willie	run	town
me	silly	fun	brown
see	Billy	sun	gown
knee	hilly	bun	crown

2 **Write words from each family on separate charts, and label the charts with the appropriate titles.** For example, *The at Family* would be the label for the words *mat, bat, cat, fat, hat*. Encourage individual students to read each word list and when they read the words correctly, write their name on the chart to show they have mastered it.

3 **Make up silly rhymes, and have the students fill in the last rhyming word.** For example, say, "My big black cat caught a little gray r…" You say the rhyme and the **r** sound, and they fill in the word *rat*.

   I climbed a tree and got stung by a b___.
   I'll run and hop till you tell me to st____.
   I like to run 'cause I think it's f___.
   I like to play on a sunny d___.

4 **On small index cards, print pairs of words from several families, one word per card.** Lay the cards out, words up, and ask the students to choose matching pairs and read the words as they choose them. For example, using eight cards, you might print *cat, bat, tin, win, hot, not, bee, see*.

5 **Using the same word cards, place them word side down, and play a game with children trying to choose two cards from the same family.** When they pick a matching pair, they keep the cards, and each word counts as one point. If they do not pick a match, they return the cards to their original position, and the next child gets to try to pick a matching pair.

6 **Divide a large piece of tag board into as many 5 inch by 7 inch boxes as possible.** This will be about 20 boxes. Write pairs of words for the families, one word per box. Lay the board on the floor. Children throw a beanbag or a coin onto the board. They try to hit two words from the same family.

7 **Write a list of common words on the board with pairs of words starting with the same letter.** Say some sentences to the class, leaving out one word but giving its beginning letter. The students must pick a word from the board that begins with the letter you give them and that also makes sense. For example, you may write the words *here, come, go, can, how, good*. Then you write a letter on the board, and tell the students they must choose one of the words that starts with that letter and makes sense in the sentence.

    Sample sentences: g   I will ask Mom if I can _____. go

                      h   I don't know ___ you do that. how

                      c   Will you _____ with me? come

   On the following page you will find a sample handout to help students reinforce their knowledge of word families. The format is simple to copy for any word family you wish to emphasize.

The "at" Family Student Handout

My name is _____.

Today is Monday   Tuesday   Wednesday   Thursday   Friday.

Find the words.

cat   bat   fat   hat   mat   pat   sat

a b c a t f m t e u
z f a t c d l m a t
p a t c g h j k l m
o b a t q r s a t u
n t h a t l s o v t

Fill in at.

The c ___ ___ s ___ ___ down.

The h ___ ___ is on the m ___ ___.

I will p___ ___ the c ___ ___.

Draw a silly picture.
The cat and the bat sat on the hat.

Chapter Four

WRITING ABOUT THE RHYMES

Learning writing skills is an integral part of learning to read, and those skills are best learned together. Linking writing to the reading process makes children think about what they have read and facilitates comprehension. Because reading without comprehension is not reading at all, working on both skills is critical to the learning process.

1 **Write the words *yes* and *no* on the board.** Begin the writing exercises by asking questions about the rhymes that can be answered by those words. *Does Mary have a lamb? Did a horse follow Mary to school one day? Did the children laugh when they saw a lamb in school? Was the lamb brown?* Ask the children to write *yes* or *no* to answer the questions.

2 **Write the names of the rhymes on the board, and give a summary of one of them at a time.** Children select from the list on the board and write the name of the rhyme, for example: *This is a story about a boy who did not do his job. He fell asleep instead.* Children write *Little Boy Blue*.

3 **Write several incomplete sentences on the board along with a list of words that can be used to complete them.** Children copy the sentences and select the correct words to complete them, for example: *Mary had a little _____. Little Boy Blue blew a _____.*

4 **Branch out into entire sentences.** Ask questions and answer them as a group. Write the response on the board to be copied. When the children have grasped the concept of a sentence, ask them to answer the questions on their own. Always ask questions that will provoke a short answer and one that can be answered by using words from the rhyme.

> What did Mary have? *Mary had a little lamb.*
> What did it make the children do when they saw the lamb in school? *It made the children laugh and play.*

5 **Ask questions that require critical thinking.** Encourage the students to sound out the words in their response and use words from the word wall. When students begin to sound out words, they will probably leave out the vowels. That is fine, as they are putting down the letters they hear. Assure them that they have written the words in a perfect way for beginning writers, and gently show them the "grown-up" way to spell the words by writing them somewhere on their paper, but not in their response.

> Why did the lamb follow Mary? *It loves her.*
> Why did the children laugh? *It is funny to see a lamb in school.*

6 **Ask questions that need to be answered by a color word in a simple sentence.**

> What color is Mary's lamb? *The lamb is white.*
> What color is the sun? *The sun is yellow.*
> What color is the sky? What color is your hair? What color is the floor?

7 **Make three charts and hang them where they can be easily seen.** On the first chart print the words *A, This,* and *The.* On the second one, paste pictures of people and animals cut from magazines and label them *dog, man, girl, boy, cat, snake,* and so on. The last chart should have pictures of actions: someone ironing, swimming, eating, dancing, flying, and so on. Label the actions *irons, swims, eats, dances, flies.* Ask the children to choose one word from each chart to make sentences. You can ask for sentences that make sense: *The man swims. The girl dances.* You can ask for silly sentences: *The fish irons. A snake dances. A fish flies.*

8 **Read a new rhyme to the class, and ask them to write a sentence telling what the rhyme is about.** An example is *Little Miss Muffet was a little girl who was scared by a spider.*

9 **On the board list the characters from the nursery rhymes.** Also write the words *I would like to be* and *I would not like to be* on the board. Ask the children to choose one of the characters and write why they would like or not like to be that person. For example, they might write *I would like to be Mary because I like lambs. I would not like to be Humpty Dumpty. I do not like to fall.*

10 **Begin some sentences on the board, and ask the children to complete them in their own words.** Some examples are *I like to _____. I can _____. My house is _____. This school is _____.*

Sample Writing Handouts

Following are four sample writing handouts. The first two are intended for students just beginning to write out their thoughts, and they include needed vocabulary. The second two are more difficult, as the children need to use their own vocabulary to write stories. It will be easy for you to copy the format of these handouts for other writing lessons that you design.

The first handout is a "fill in the blank" story with the necessary vocabulary listed. The second handout also lists vocabulary, but it asks the students to create a story using those words and any they want to add. The third handout has random shapes that the students can turn into any picture they like and then write a story about the picture. For instance they may think the shapes are stars, comets, shields for knights, spiky hair, or paint spills. The fourth handout asks the student to make compound words and then use those words in a short story about a specific topic.

NOTE: A good way to introduce a new concept, such as making compound words, is to explain the concept to the children, demonstrate how to use the concept, practice with the children, and then have the children practice on their own.

Step One: Explain to the students what a compound word is. Show several examples.

Step Two: On the board, write two lists of words that can be used to make compound words. Demonstrate how the words are joined to make compound words.

Step Three: Put two more lists of words on the board that can be joined to make compound words. Together, you and the children make compound words.

Step Four: Give each student a handout, or put two more lists of words on the board. Ask the students to make compound words. Check the students' work together, and note any misunderstandings or errors to see whether a review lesson is needed.

Writing Student Handout #1

My name is _____.

Today is _____.

Use the words to make a story.

cat	beach	swim	come	great
dog	track	play	go	good
boy	park	run	play	bad

One day a _____ went to the _____.

He wanted to _____.

He saw a friend.

The friend said, "I want to _____ with you."

The _____ and his friend had a _____ time.

Draw a picture that shows what happens in your story.

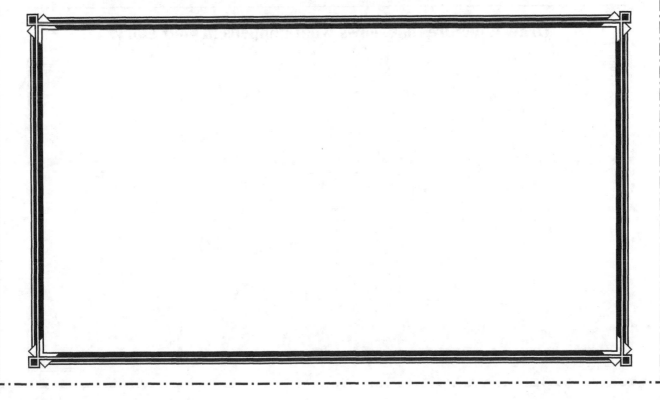

Writing Student Handout #2

My name is _____.

Today is _____.

Use the words to help you write a story about a clown.
Use some of your own words, too.

big	bike	blue	circus	clown	happy
hat	laughed	little	monkey	red	rides
sad	shoes	tent	tricks	white	yellow

_____

_____

_____

_____

_____

_____

_____

Draw a picture that shows what happens in your story.

Writing Student Handout #3

My name is _____.

Today is _____.

Draw a picture with these two things. What can they be?

Write a story about the picture you made. _____

_____

_____

_____

_____

_____

_____

_____

_____

Writing Student Handout #4

My name is _____.

Today is _____.

Put the words together to make bigger words. Write the words here.

in	house	_____
dog	out	_____
with	to	_____
fire	self	_____
my	fighter	_____

Write a story about a firefighter and his or her dog. What do they do? Use the words you made.

_____

_____

_____

_____

_____

_____

_____

_____

_____

_____

_____

Developing a Basic Sight Word Vocabulary

The basic vocabulary for the four interactive plays and the short plays that follow is made up largely of words from the list of most frequently used words in the English language. It is important that children have ample time to read and practice these words through work and play. Analyze any paragraph from any book, and you will see that most of the words are from this basic list. It makes sense that once children master these words, their reading develops quickly

The words were compiled by Edward William Dolch in his book *Problems in Reading,* so the list is often called the Dolch list.

If you study any piece of writing, you will see some of the most commonly used words in the English language. Look at the preceding sentence. You see *if, you, any, of, will, see, what, some, of, the, in, are.* These are some of the words your students must learn by sight if they are to progress in their reading skills. When readers recognize these words immediately, they do not have to stop and decode them. They can concentrate on words they do not know.

For more information about the Dolch words and for a complete list of the words, type *Dolch words* in the search box on your Internet screen. You will be directed to several sites and be able to print copies of the list. One of these sites is: <http://gemini.es.brevard.k12.fl.us/sheppard/reading/dolch.html>.

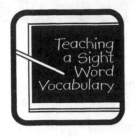

Chapter Five

TEACHING A BASIC SIGHT WORD VOCABULARY

The best way to learn the Dolch words is through seeing them in context, but there are many enjoyable games that help children learn the words by sight. Here are some suggestions for teaching the words so they become a part of the student's basic sight vocabulary. Add these classroom tested ideas to your favorite activities.

1 **Use flash cards.**

2 **Make games.** Print each word on two small cards, and then place the cards with the words facing down. Turning two cards over at a time, players must try to pair matching cards. If they turn up a match, they keep the cards and score two points; if they don't turn up a match, they turn the cards over and return them to the table for the next player's turn.

3 **Put several of the words on a chart next to the door.** Each time the students line up to leave the room, read the words aloud, or ask individual students to point to different words for their release ticket. Change the words as they are learned.

4 **Place the words on a word wall.** Use them when writing stories.

5 **Play "Find Your Partner."** Write each word on two separate cards, and distribute the cards to the class. Children must find the other class member whose word matches theirs.

6 **Play "Make a Sentence."** Write the words on cards enough times to make several sentences. Children find other class members whose words will combine with theirs to make a sentence. Then they stand in the order of the sentence so that others can read their words, for example: *I will go. I can help. I am big. I see you.*

7 **Play a beanbag game.** Use a tag board chart like the one you made for learning word families. Divide the tag board into about 20 5-inch by 7-inch boxes. Write a word in each box, and put the chart on the floor. Children toss a bean bag or coin. If they know the word the bag or coin falls on, they get a point. Tally the points to see who has ended up as first winner, second winner, third winner, and so on.

8 **Write mixed up sentences on the board for the children to unscramble.** Examples are *can go I, big am I.*

9 **Make individual books with simple sentences for the children to illustrate.** Fold a paper into four boxes so it makes a little book. Write a simple sentence in each box. Unfold the paper and make a copy for each child. Show them how to refold the paper to make their own little book. Then they can read the sentences and draw pictures to go with the story. Words are included here that are not on the list of most commonly used words in the English language because they are words that evoke pictures, such as *cat, dog,* and *ball.* Some examples are a) *I see a black cat. I can play with the cat. The cat can jump. The cat went away.* b) *A big dog ran to me. I played with the dog. I gave the dog a bone. He ate it.*

10 **Play an active reading game.** On one side of the room put a large sign that says *I like it.* On the other side of the room, put a sign that says *I do not like it.* Then ask the children questions that can be answered by either of the two written statements, for example, *Do you like chocolate ice cream?* The children must answer the questions by standing by the sign that tells how they feel. This is an active game that's good to play when the children have been sitting for awhile. Other signs can be *I can do it* and *I cannot do it* for skills such as setting the table, driving a car, running the washing machine, and writing their name. The signs *I know how to play it* and *I do not know how to play it* can be used for lists of games and activities. Make sure to put the periods after the sentences.

11 **Choose words that make sense.** Draw pictures on the board or on a piece of chart paper. Then write two sentences, one of which describes the picture. For example, draw a picture of a little ball. Write the sentences *This is a big ball. This is a little ball.* The children have to choose the right sentence.

12 **Search for words.** Print a story on chart paper. Ask the children to find specific words in the story and circle them. See how many times each word is there. If they search for several words in the same story, each different word can be circled with a different color. For instance, every time the word *all* is seen, it can be circled with a red crayon, *big* with a blue crayon, and so on.

13 **Make sentences.** Divide the class into small groups of three or four. Working with two groups at a time, give each group a set of four or five index cards with words on them that will make a complete sentence. One child at a time brings the cards up to the board and arranges them in the right order. Then the child reads the sentence, shuffles the cards, and gives them to the next child in his or her group. Each child in the group repeats the actions until all have had a turn. To make the game less competitive, have the students compete against the clock, instead of against another group, by giving them a time when they must be done, such as five or ten minutes. Sample sentences are *The big dog is brown. She likes to jump down. They will take the cat. I will call my mom.*

14 **Send a list of the words you are emphasizing home with the students.** Include some suggestions for how parents can help their children learn the words.

Interactive Plays

Each of the following four chapters is a complete interactive play that provides an opportunity for students to practice basic sight words and phonic skills in a critical thinking activity.

Each play has roles for five actors and one narrator. The actors read answers from answer sheets in response to questions posed by the narrator. Based on the answers given, the audience (the rest of the class) then tries to guess how the actors feel about certain foods or activities.

Each play is followed by a whole language extension activity and a student handout.

How to Use This Section

1 **Copy the answer sheets for play number one, *I Do Not Like It,* and cut them on the dotted lines so you have five separate answer sheets.** Paste each on a piece of construction paper. On the opposite side of the answers, number the sheets according to the number of the answer sheet from one to five. The result will be the answer sheet on one side and a large number on the other. This will enable the audience to identify each actor by number.

2 **Explain to the children that they will be taking turns acting in a play.** Tell them that they will read answers to questions you ask by reading a sentence on the paper you will give them.

3 **For each play choose five children to be the actors, and give them a number from one to five.** Give each actor the answer sheet corresponding to his or her number. Line up the actors in the front of the class in numerical order.

4 **Follow the directions that accompany and follow each interactive play, and have fun!** The suggested whole language extension activities that follow each play are related to the topic of the play and encourage critical thinking skills.

5 **Complete the included student handout together.** To reinforce skills, complete the student handouts together, and send them home with students for reading practice.

Chapter Six

I DO NOT LIKE IT!

I n this interactive play, the students must guess which actor in the play likes or dislikes certain foods.

Choose five children to be the actors, and give them a number from one to five. Cut the answer sheets that follow on the dotted line and paste them each on a piece of construction paper, and give each actor the answer sheet corresponding to his or her number. Line up the actors in the front of the class in numerical order.

Vocabulary

Practice these words before starting the activity:
I will go with you no yes to the store not

Narrator: We are going to play a guessing game. As you can see, there are five children here. One child does not like pizza, one does not like ice cream, one does not like candy, one does not like spinach, and one does not like juice. Your job is to discover which child is which. *(As you say them, print the words* pizza, ice cream, candy, spinach *and* juice *on the board or chart so the class can see them.)* I am going to ask these children some questions and after all of them have answered, I will ask you to take some guesses. Are you ready?

I must go to the store to buy something that has green leaves. Who will go with me? *(Explain to the players that they should read only the words that are printed after the number 1 on their answer sheet.)*

Number 1: I will go with you.
Number 2: I will go with you.
Number 3: No, I will not go with you.
Number 4: Yes, I will go.
Number 5: I will go with you to the store.

Narrator: Who does not want to go to the store with me? *(Wait for an answer. Have the players repeat their answers if necessary.)* Right, Number 3 does not want to go to the store with me. What doesn't Number 3 like? *(spinach) (If the class cannot guess, repeat the words on the board, and remind them that you are going to get something that has green leaves. Ask a child to go to the board and circle the word* spinach. *Use the beginning letter as a clue. Repeat the words on the board as often as necessary.)*

I am going out to dinner. I am hungry for something with cheese and tomato sauce on it. Who will go with me? *(Players read the words after the number 2.)*

Number 1: I will go.
Number 2: I will not go.
Number 3: Yes, I will go with you.
Number 4: I will go with you.
Number 5: I will go with you to the store.

Narrator: What am I going to have for dinner? *(pizza)* Who does not like pizza? *(Number 2)* *(Ask a child to go to the board and circle the word* pizza.*)*

I am going to buy something that is cold and sweet. I will have to eat it quickly before it melts. Who wants to go with me? *(Players read the words after the number 3.)*

Number 1: No, no. I will not go.
Number 2: I will go to the store.
Number 3: Yes, I will go with you.
Number 4: I will go with you.
Number 5: Yes, I will go.

Narrator: What am I going to buy at the store? *(ice cream)* Who does not like ice cream? *(Number 1)* *(Ask a child to circle the words* ice cream.*)*

I am very thirsty. I will go to the store to buy something that I like to drink that is made from fruit. Who wants to go with me? *(Players read the words after the number 4.)*

Number 1: I will go with you.
Number 2: I will go with you.
Number 3: Yes, I will go to the store.
Number 4: Yes, I will go to the store.
Number 5: No, I will not go with you.

Narrator: What am I going to buy? *(juice)* Which child does not like juice? *(Number 5)* *(Ask a child to circle the word* juice *on the board.)*

I am going to the store to buy something sweet. It has chocolate and nuts in it, and comes wrapped in paper. Who will go with me? *(Players read the words after the number 5.)*

Number 1: I will go with you.
Number 2: Yes, I will go.
Number 3: I will go to the store.
Number 4: No, no, I will not go.
Number 5: I will go with you.

Narrator: What am I going to the store to buy? *(candy)* Who does not like candy? *(Number 4)* *(Ask a child to circle the word* candy *on the board.)*

Now let's see who can remember which child didn't like each item. *(Point to the circled words one at a time.)* Who didn't like spinach? *(Number 3)* Who didn't like pizza? *(Number 2)* Who didn't like ice cream? *(Number 1)* Who didn't like juice? *(Number 5)* Who didn't like

I Do Not Like It! Answer Sheets

Answer Sheet

Play Number 1
I Do Not Like It!
Actor Number 1

1. I will go with you.
2. I will go.
3. No, no. I will not go.
4. I will go with you.
5. I will go with you.

Answer Sheet

Play Number 1
I Do Not Like It!
Actor Number 2

1. I will go with you.
2. I will not go.
3. I will go to the store.
4. I will go with you.
5. Yes, I will go.

Answer Sheet

Play Number 1
I Do Not Like It!
Actor Number 3

1. No, I will not go with you.
2. Yes, I will go with you.
3. Yes, I will go with you.
4. Yes, I will go to the store.
5. I will go to the store.

Answer Sheet

Play Number 1
I Do Not Like It!
Actor Number 4

1. Yes, I will go.
2. I will go with you.
3. I will go with you.
4. Yes, I will go to the store.
5. No, no, I will not go.

Answer Sheet

Play Number 1
I Do Not Like It!
Actor Number 5

1. I will go with you to the store.
2. I will go with you to the store.
3. Yes, I will go.
4. No, I will not go with you.
5. I will go with you.

I Do Not Like It!
☑ Extension Activities ★ ★

1. Ask the students to name, describe, and draw or find pictures of other food items that can be bought at the store. Help the class put the foods named into classifications. Write them on a wall chart. Attach their illustrations. Some examples are *cereal, bread, and doughnuts are grains;* and *pork chops, steak, and hot dogs are meat.* Read the chart together as a class activity.

2. Build a bar graph by attaching two pages of one-inch bar graph paper sideways with one food listed in the first box on one line and another listed in the first box on another line. The children write their names in a box beside the food they prefer, leaving no blank boxes between names. After all have had a chance to write their names in a box, shade the boxes with names in them to make a simple bar graph showing which food is preferred more often. You can repeat this activity several times using different foods or choices from other areas, such as games or books.

3. Ask the children to draw a picture of their favorite thing to buy at the store and write *I like it.* under the picture. Play a guessing game. Each child describes his or her favorite thing to the class before showing the picture. The class tries to guess what it is.

I Like It!

Abby	Jacob	Daniel

Adam	Bobby	Pam	Chris

Alex	Annie

I Do Not Like It!
Student Handout

My name is _____.

Today is Monday   Tuesday   Wednesday   Thursday   Friday.

If you like what is in the picture, write *will go*.
If you do not like what is in the picture, write *will not go*.

Banana

   I _____ to the store.
           will go   will not go

ice cream

   I _____ to the store.
           will go   will not go

carrot

   I _____ to the store.
           will go   will not go

What do you like at the store?_____

_____.

What do you <u>not</u> like at the store? _____

_____.

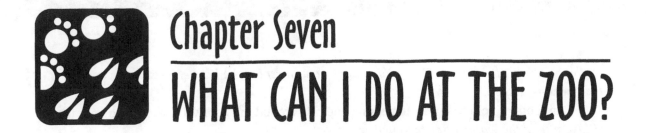

Chapter Seven
WHAT CAN I DO AT THE ZOO?

In this interactive play, the students must use clues to answer questions about favorite activities and animals at the zoo. There are five players and a narrator.

Choose five children to be the actors, and give them a number from one to five. Cut the answer sheets that follow on the dotted line, and give each actor the answer sheet corresponding to his or her number. Line up the actors in the front of the class in numerical order.

This play includes vocabulary from the previous play in addition to new vocabulary.

Vocabulary

Review words: I will go with you no yes to the store not
New vocabulary: Practice these words before starting the activity:
can cannot see a at something like look come get big stay here do

Narrator: We are going to play a guessing game. As you can see, there are five children here. Each of them likes to do something special at the zoo. Your job is to discover what each child likes best. Here are some of the things they like to do. *(Write on the board* feed the birds, see the bears, look at the lions, ride the camel, pet the baby animals *as you read the phrases. This would be a good time to have a discussion of what the students like to do at the zoo. Ask if they like to do any of the things on the list that you have written.)*

I am going to ask these children some questions and after all of them have answered, I will ask you to take some guesses. Are you ready?

I am going to buy something for some little animals to eat. Who wants to come with me? *(Explain to the players that they should read only the words that are printed after the number 1 on the answer sheet.)*

Number 1: I will come with you to get something.
Number 2: I will not get something.
Number 3: No, I will stay here.
Number 4: I cannot come to get something.
Number 5: I do not like to get something.

Narrator: Who wants to go with me to get something? *(Number 1)* Why are we going to buy something? *(to feed the birds)* What do you think we will buy to feed them? *(seeds, corn, bread)* What does Number 1 like to do at the zoo? *(Feed the birds.)* (Ask a child from the class to go to the board and circle the phrase feed the birds. Use beginning letters as clues. Repeat the words* *on the board as often as necessary. You might want to repeat the list before starting each part of the guessing game.)*

I am going to climb up on something and ride around the zoo. Who will come with me? *(Players read the words after the number 2.)*

Number 1: I will stay here.
Number 2: I cannot come with you.
Number 3: I like to get on something. I will come.
Number 4: No, I will not come with you.
Number 5: I do not like to get on something.

Narrator: What am I going to do? *(ride the camel) (Reread the board list, if necessary.)* Who wants to come with me? *(Number 3) (Ask a child to go to the board and circle the words* ride the camel.*)*

I am going to see some animals that like to roar very loudly. Who wants to come with me? *(Players read the words after the number 3.)*

Number 1: I do not like to go.
Number 2: I will not come with you.
Number 3: No, no. I cannot come with you.
Number 4: I will go look with you.
Number 5: I will not go with you to see something.

Narrator: What animal on our list roars the loudest? *(lions)* What am I going to do? *(look at the lions)* Who will come with me? *(Number 4)* What does Number 4 like to do at the zoo? *(look at the lions) (Ask a child to circle those words on the board.)*

I am going to do something with some very young animals. Who will come with me? *(Players read the words after the number 4.)*

Number 1: I will stay here.
Number 2: I cannot go with you to do something.
Number 3: I do not like to come with you.
Number 4: I will not go with you to do something.
Number 5: I will come with you to do something.

Narrator: Who will come with me? *(Number 5)* What animals will we see? *(baby animals)* What will we do? *(pet the baby animals) (Ask someone to circle the words* pet the baby animals.*)*

I want to see some big animals—some big, white animals. Who will come with me? *(Players read the words after the number 5.)*

Number 1: No, no. I will not come with you.
Number 2: I like something big. I will come with you.
Number 3: I cannot come with you to look.
Number 4: I will not come with you. I do not like something big.
Number 5: I will stay here. I will not come with you.

Narrator: What am I going to do? *(see the bears)* Who likes bears? *(Number 2)* *(Ask a child to circle the words* see the bears *on the board.)* I said that I am going to see the big white bears. Are all bears white? *(No, some are brown and some are black.)*

Let's see who can remember what each child wanted to do at the zoo. Who wanted to feed the birds? *(Number 1)* Who wanted to ride a camel? *(Number 3)* Who wanted to look at lions? *(Number 4)* Who wanted to pet the baby animals? *(Number 5)* Who wanted to see the bears? *(Number 2)*

What Can I Do at the Zoo? Answer Sheets

Answer Sheet

Play Number 2
What Can I Do at the Zoo?
Actor Number 1

1. I will come with you to get something.
2. I will stay here.
3. I do not like to go.
4. I will stay here.
5. No, no, I will not come with you.

Answer Sheet

Play Number 2
What Can I Do at the Zoo?
Actor Number 2

1. I will not get something.
2. I cannot come with you.
3. I will not come with you.
4. I cannot go with you to do something.
5. I like something big. I will come with you.

Answer Sheet

Play Number 2
What Can I Do at the Zoo?
Actor Number 3

1. No, I will stay here.
2. I like to get on something. I will come.
3. No, no. I cannot come with you.
4. I do not like to come with you.
5. I cannot come with you to look.

Answer Sheet

Play Number 2
What Can I Do at the Zoo?
Actor Number 4

1. I cannot come to get something.
2. No, I will not come with you.
3. I will go look with you.
4. I will not go with you to do something.
5. I will not come with you. I do not like something big.

Answer Sheet

Play Number 2
What Can I Do at the Zoo?
Actor Number 5

1. I do not like to get something.
2. I do not like to get on something.
3. I will not go with you to see something.
4. I will come with you to do something.
5. I will stay here. I will not come with you.

What Can I Do at the Zoo?
★ ★ Extension Activities ★ ★

1   Using the phrases on the board from the last play (feed the birds, ride a camel, look at lions, pet the baby animals, see the bears), ask each child to vote for one activity that would be their favorite and explain why they chose it. Make a graph showing how many students chose each zoo activity. There are several ways to vote: 1) the children can raise their hands when the activity they choose is read; 2) there can be a written ballot with children tallying the votes and reading what activities have been chosen; 3) the students can put a mark after the activity they choose, and the marks can be counted to see how many have chosen each activity.

2   Make a mural by having children draw zoo pictures and attaching them to a large piece of paper. Then ask the class to call out all the zoo words they can think of. Write the words randomly on the mural. Each day refer to the mural, and ask the children to choose zoo words and put them together in sentences for writing practice.

3   Encourage children to tell stories about when they visited the zoo. If they have never visited a zoo, ask them to tell why they think they would or would not like to visit one. Write one sentence about each child's story on a chart, for example:
Lisa saw a black and orange tiger.
Chris petted a baby lamb.
Ellen laughed at the monkeys.
Marc wants to go to the zoo to see the elephants squirt water.

4   Use the chart for reading practice. For instance, you could ask a child to read another student's sentence, for example: *Chris, what did Lisa see at the zoo? Marc, what made Ellen laugh?*

VOTE!
☑ Feed the birds
☐ Ride a camel
☐ Look at lions
☐ Pet the baby animals
☐ See the bears

What Can I Do at the Zoo?
Student Handout

My name is _____.

Today is Monday   Tuesday   Wednesday   Thursday   Friday.

Match the little words to make big words.
Write the words here.

some	not	_____
in	thing	_____
can	to	_____
may	round	_____
a	be	_____

Put the words in the right order.

cannot I pet lion the _____.

to see want I monkeys the _____.

I Maybe can the ducks feed _____.

will walk We around zoo the _____.

bears The into went cave the _____.

What do you like at the zoo?

_____.

Chapter Eight
GAMES I CAN PLAY

I n this interactive play, children must guess which games the actors enjoy. The vocabulary in this play includes words practiced in the previous plays in addition to new vocabulary.

There are five players and a narrator. Choose five children to be the actors, and give them a number from one to five. Cut the answer sheets that follow on the dotted line, and give each actor the answer sheet corresponding to his or her number. Line up the actors in the front of the class in numerical order.

Vocabulary

Review words: I will go with you no yes to the store not can cannot see a at like look come get big stay here do something
New vocabulary: Practice these words before starting the activity:
ball play game team Mom Dad friend school run fast but

Narrator: We are going to play a guessing game. There are five children here. They all like to play games, but each one has a favorite game. One likes soccer, one likes football, one likes baseball, one likes tennis, and one likes ice hockey. *(Write these words on the board as you say them. You may want to make sure the children are familiar with the games.)* Your job will be to discover which child likes which game.

I am going to ask these children some questions and after all of them have answered, I will ask you to take some guesses. Are you ready?

I want to play a game where I can hit a ball very, very far, and score a home run for my team. Who wants to play with me? *(Players read the words after the number 1.)*

Number 1: I do not like to hit a ball. I will go to the store.
Number 2: I will play with the team and hit a ball. I like to play ball.
Number 3: No, I do not play with a ball. I will play a game with a friend.
Number 4: I cannot play with you. I will stay here with Dad.
Number 5: I can come with you, but I will not play the game.

Narrator: Who will play with me? *(Number 2)* What game will we play? *(baseball)* *(Ask a child to circle the word* baseball *on the board.)*

I am going to the ice skating rink to play a game. I will hit a puck and try to score a point for my team. Who will play with me? *(Players read the words after the number 2.)*

Number 1: I like to play ball. I will play a ball game with a friend.
Number 2: I do not like to play. I will go to the store with Mom.
Number 3: You will play a game I like. I can play the game with you.
Number 4: Dad and I will play a game with a ball.
Number 5: I like to play something with a ball. You will not play with a ball.

Narrator: What game will I play? *(ice hockey)* Is there someone who will play ice hockey with me? *(Number 3) (Ask someone to circle the words* ice hockey *on the board.)* What did some of the other children like to play? *(They like ball games.)*

    I am going to play a game where I have to run very fast with a ball. I have to be careful that no one tackles me. I want to score a touchdown for my team. Who will play with me? *(Players read the words after the number 3.)*

Number 1: I will go to the store with Dad. I will look at something at the store.
Number 2: Mom and I will stay here. We cannot come.
Number 3: I do not like to run fast with a ball.
Number 4: I can run fast. I can play a game with a ball and run fast.
Number 5: A friend and I will play something here.

Narrator: What is the name of the game where you run very fast with a ball and try to score a touchdown? *(football)* Is there someone here who likes football and will play with me? *(Number 4) (Ask someone to go to the board and circle the word* football.*)*

    I have a racquet to hit a ball over a net. I need a friend to play with me. Who will it be? *(Players read the words after the number 4.)*

Number 1: I can play ball. I can be a friend.
Number 2: I cannot play. I will do something here with Mom.
Number 3: Dad and I will play ball here.
Number 4: I will go to the store and see something big.
Number 5: A friend and I will go to play something at the store.

Narrator: What game can be played by two people hitting a ball over a net? *(tennis)* Who likes tennis here? *(Number 1) (Ask someone to circle the word* tennis *on the board.)*

    I like to kick a ball and run down the field to score a goal. Who will play with me and my team? *(Players read the words after the number 5.)*

Number 1: You will play a game with a ball. I will do something here.
Number 2: I do not like to run. I will play a game with a friend.
Number 3: You are my friend, but I do not like to play ball.
Number 4: I cannot run fast. I like to play something here.
Number 5: I can run fast. I will play ball with you.

Narrator: What game will I play with my team? *(soccer)* Who will play with me? *(Number 5) (Ask someone to circle the word* soccer *on the board.)*

Games I Can Play Answer Sheets

Answer Sheet

Play Number 3
Games I Can Play
Actor Number 1

1. I do not like to hit a ball. I will go to the store.
2. I like to play ball. I will play a ball game with a friend.
3. I will go to the store with Dad. I will look at something at the store.
4. I can play with a ball. I can be a friend.
5. You will play a game with a ball. I will do something here.

Answer Sheet

Play Number 3
Games I Can Play
Actor Number 2

1. I will play with the team and hit a ball. I like to play ball.
2. I do not like to play. I will go to the store with Mom.
3. Mom and I will stay here. We cannot come.
4. I cannot play. I will do something here with Mom.
5. I do not like to run. I will play a game with a friend.

Answer Sheet

Play Number 3
Games I Can Play
Actor Number 3

1. No, I do not play with a ball. I will play a game with a friend.
2. You will play a game I like. I can play the game with you.
3. I do not like to run fast with a ball.
4. Dad and I will play ball here.
5. You are my friend, but I do not like to play ball.

Answer Sheet

Play Number 3
Games I Can Play
Actor Number 4

1. I cannot play with you. I will stay here with Dad.
2. Dad and I will play a game with a ball.
3. I can run fast. I can play a game with a ball and run fast.
4. I will go to the store and see something big.
5. I cannot run fast. I like to play something here.

Answer Sheet

Play Number 3
Games I Can Play
Actor Number 5

1. I can come with you, but I will not play the game.
2. I like to play something with a ball. You will not play with a ball.
3. A friend and I will play something here.
4. A friend and I will go to play something at the store.
5. I can run fast. I will play ball with you.

Games I Can Play

★ ★ ✔ Extension Activities ★ ★

1 Discuss and chart major components of each sport in three columns. Add any other games the class suggests.

Name of Game	What you need to play the game	How you play the game
Tennis	racquet, net, court	hit a ball over the net

2 Ask each child to secretly choose a sport, draw an illustration, and write a simple sentence about it. Then each child can pantomime the sport. When the rest of the class has guessed the sport, the student can read his or her sentence aloud. The pictures and sentences can be posted on a bulletin board along with the sports chart and used for reading practice.

Games I Can Play
Student Handout

My name is _____.

Today is Monday   Tuesday   Wednesday   Thursday   Friday.

Read the words. See how fast you can climb the steps.

<u>into</u>   <u>here</u>

  <u>mom</u>   <u>see</u>

    <u>game</u>   <u>long</u>

      <u>ball</u>   <u>stay</u>

        <u>play</u>   <u>like</u>

          <u>big</u>   <u>look</u>

        <u>something</u>   <u>but</u>

What words can you find?	**Put in the missing letters.**	
i n t o h f g m o m	h ___ r e	se ___
x y z g a m e r s t	l ___ ng	st ___ ___
t b a l l g h j b i g	l ___ ke	l ___ ___ k
u v p l a y m s e e	b ___ t	b ___ g
s o m e t h i n g w	pl ___ ___	b ___ ll

What is the game you like best? Tell how you play that game.

_____

_____

_____.

Chapter Nine

I CAN SHOP

In this interactive play children must guess what items the actors will buy at the store. The play includes vocabulary from the three previous plays in addition to new vocabulary.

There are five players and a narrator. Choose five children to be the actors, and give them a number from one to five. Cut the answer sheets that follow on the dotted line, and give each actor the answer sheet corresponding to his or her number. Line up the actors in the front of the class in numerical order.

Vocabulary

Review words: I will go with you no yes to the store not can cannot see a at like look come get big stay here do something Dad friend school run fast but ball play game team Mom

New vocabulary: Practice these words before starting the activity: shop red blue brown green purple orange black white buy new my for me good that soft

Narrator: We are going to play a guessing game. There are five children here. They are all going shopping. One will buy a brown teddy bear, one will buy a big, red truck, one will buy a doll with black hair, one will buy some sweet candy, and one will buy brand new shoes. *(Write the items the children will buy on the board as you say their names. Notice that each of the phrases to be written on the board contains one blend: br, tr, bl, sw, and one digraph sh. Point these out to the students.)* I am going to ask the children some questions and after all of them have answered, I will ask you to take some guesses. Are you ready?

I am looking at something that is little. I can play with it. I can dress it in a pretty dress and shiny shoes. Who wants to buy this toy? *(Players read the words after the number 1.)*

Number 1: I like something big. I do not like something little.
Number 2: Mom and I will not buy something that is little.
Number 3: I like something big that can go fast.
Number 4: I like something little. I like to play with something little.
Number 5: I do not want to buy the little toy. I want a big toy.

Narrator: What are we going to buy? *(a doll with black hair)* Who wants to buy the doll? *(Number 4)* What will Number 4 do with the doll? *(various responses) (Ask a child to circle the*

five words a doll with black hair *on the board.)*

I am going to the store to shop. We will buy something new to wear. Who wants to come with me? (*Players read the words after the number 2.*)

Number 1: I like something new, but I will play here with a friend.
Number 2: I do not want something new. I will play ball with Dad.
Number 3: I want something new. I will like something new for me.
Number 4: I will stay here with Mom. We will play a game.
Number 5: You go to the store. I want to do something with my friend.

Narrator: What will we buy at the store? (*brand new shoes*) Who wants to buy new shoes? (*Number 3*) What kind of shoes do you think Number 3 will want to buy? (*various responses*) Why might Number 3 need new shoes? (*various responses*) (*Ask a child to circle the words* brand new shoes *on the board.)*

I am hungry for something. I would like something sugary. Who wants to come with me? (*Players read the words after the number 3.*)

Number 1: I do not want to stay here. I will like something to eat.
Number 2: I cannot come. I will stay here. I will help Mom.
Number 3: I like something to eat, but I will play a game here.
Number 4: Can you stay here with me? I cannot go.
Number 5: Dad and I will play something here.

Narrator: What am I going to buy? (*sweet candy*) Who likes sweet candy? (*Numbers 1 and 3*) Who will come with me? (*Number 1*) (*Ask someone to circle the words* sweet candy.*) Does any-one here like candy? Tell me about the kinds you like. (*List the names of the candy the children like. Read the list together a few times.*)

I am going to the store to pick out something to play with. It can go fast on its four black wheels. Who will go with me? (*Players read the words after the number 4.*)

Number 1: I like something that can go fast, but I must eat now.
Number 2: I will ask Mom if I can come. I like a toy that can go fast.
Number 3: Dad's car has four wheels. It can go fast. I will go with Dad.
Number 4: Will you play with me when you come home? I must stay here.
Number 5: Mom and I will work at home now.

Narrator: Who wants to go with me? (*Number 2*) What will we get? (*a red truck*) (*Ask a child to circle the words* a red truck.*) Can Number 2 come with me for sure? (*if his or her Mom*

says yes)

I am going to the store to buy something I can take to bed with me. It is soft and brown, and I like to hug it. Who will come with me? (*Players read the words after the number 5.*)

Number 1: I do not want something now. I like to play now.
Number 2: I will go with Dad and Mom to the store.
Number 3: I want to go, but Dad says I cannot go with you.
Number 4: I like something fast to play with.
Number 5: I like something soft and brown. Can my friend come, too?

Narrator: What am I going to buy at the store? (*teddy bear*) Who will come with me? (*Number 5*) (*Ask someone to circle the words* teddy bear *on the board.*)

I Can Shop Answer Sheets

Answer Sheet

Play Number 4
I Can Shop
Actor Number 1

1. I like something big. I do not like something little.
2. I like something new, but I will play here with a friend.
3. I do not want to stay here. I will like something to eat.
4. I like something that can go fast, but I must eat now.
5. I do not want something now. I like to play now.

Answer Sheet

Play Number 4
I Can Shop
Actor Number 2

1. Mom and I will not buy something that is little.
2. I do not want something new. I will play ball with Dad.
3. I cannot come. I will stay here. I will help Mom.
4. I will ask Mom if I can come. I like a toy that can go fast.
5. I will go with Dad and Mom to the store.

Answer Sheet

Play Number 4
I Can Shop
Actor Number 3

1. I like something big that can go fast.
2. I want something new. I will like something new for me.
3. I like something to eat, but I will play a game here.
4. Dad's car has four wheels. It can go fast. I will go with Dad.
5. I want to go, but Dad says I cannot go with you.

Answer Sheet

Play Number 4
I Can Shop
Actor Number 4

1. I like something little. I like to play with something little.
2. I will stay here with Mom. We will play a game.
3. Can you stay here with me? I cannot go.
4. Will you play with me when you come home? I must stay here.
5. I like something fast to play with.

Answer Sheet

Play Number 4
I Can Shop
Actor Number 5

1. I do not want to buy the little toy. I want a big toy.
2. You go to the store. I want to do something with my friend.
3. Dad and I will play something here.
4. Mom and I will work at home now.
5. I like something soft and brown. Can my friend come, too?

I Can Shop
✔ Extension Activities
★ ★ ★ ★

1 Elicit names of other toys from the class. Put the name and a picture of each toy at the top of separate pieces of paper. Make a pattern book by using the following familiar rhyme:

> At the store, what do you see? I see some dolls smiling at me.
> At the store, what do you see? I see some trucks zooming to me.
> At the store, what do you see? I see some tops twirling round me.

2 Assemble a library of books about toys. Assign one to each child or pair of children, give them time to look through the book, and ask them to tell the class what the book is about. Many will not be able to read the books, but they can make up a story that follows the pictures.

3 Put a toy in a paper bag without letting the children see what it is. Ask them to write a guess about what the toy is, telling about its size, color, and what it can do. For instance, someone might guess that it is a baby doll that can cry and say mama, and is wearing pink pajamas. After all have shared their guesses, ask someone to take the toy from the bag.

I Can Shop
Student Handout

My name is _____.

Today is Monday   Tuesday   Wednesday   Thursday   Friday.

Colors: red blue yellow green orange purple brown black white

Answer in a whole sentence.

What color is the sky? _____.

What color is grass? _____.

What color is your hair? _____.

What color is a fire truck? _____.

What color do you like best? _____.

Write a story about your favorite toy.
Tell what color it is, how big it is,
and how you play with the toy.

Draw your toy here.

_____

_____

_____

_____

_____

_____

_____

_____

Section Four

The Play's the Thing

Included in this section are four short plays meant to be performed in readers' theater style. The children do not memorize the lines; they read them. The total number of characters in all the plays is 20. This will enable you to divide your class into four groups and assign a play to each group. If your students number more than 20, ask some students to announce the plays. The first play is short; it is a good play to assign to those students whose reading skill is progressing at a slower pace.

Each play is followed by a student handout that reviews phonic skills, emphasizes basic sight words, provokes critical thinking, and provides practice in putting thoughts into words.

How To Use This Section

1 **Read the play to the students before giving them a copy.** Read with all the expression you want them to apply when it is their turn to read. Pause midway through the reading, and ask the students to predict what they think will happen. Write their predictions on the board so you can check to see if any are correct after you finish reading the play.

2 **Copy and distribute the play to the students.** Each child should have a copy. Even though only a few students will present the play, all the children can practice it at school, and then take it home and read it to their parents.

3 **Read the play through several times with different students taking the parts each time.** After each reading, ask questions to see if the children understand what they are reading. *Why did the man think the mouse couldn't help him? What kind of an animal was the lion? Why was the lion afraid? What made the mouse's voice so loud? Why did the poor man want some pie? Why didn't the baker want to give him any pie? Was the judge fair? Where did the four friends want to go? Why did they want to go?*

4 **Demonstrate how to complete the student handout before distributing it.** Review how to complete the handout with the students. Then explain that the questions should be answered in complete sentences, and the sentences should be written in a logical order so they make sense. Demonstrate by answering the questions on the handouts yourself before giving the sheets to the class, and explain what thought processes led you to choose the order of your sentences.

For instance, after the first play, the children are asked the question *How did the man's feelings abut the mouse change in the story?* As a class, decide if his feelings changed. *How and why did they change?* Then you show that first you must write how the man felt at the beginning of the story, what made him change his mind, and then how he felt at the end of the story. An example of this is *First the man thought a little mouse could not help a big man. Then the mouse scared away a lion. The lion was going to eat the man. At the end the man knew the mouse could help him.*

5 **Distribute the student handout for students to do individually.** After the handouts are completed, ask students to share their answers with the class. Ask the students to draw on the back of the handout a picture of something that happened in the play and label the picture with a complete sentence, for example: *The lion wants to eat the man. The poor man wants a pie. The farmer stole the money.*

6 **Follow the preceding steps for all the plays before choosing students to perform in them.** After all the plays are read, ask for volunteers for each play. Give time for actors to practice, and make simple costumes if you like: a yellow crepe paper mane for the lion, black construction paper whiskers for the mouse, a cap and toy gun for the hunter, a chef's cap or apron for the baker, a bandanna tied on a stick for the poor man, drawings of musical instruments for the musicians, and so on.

7 **Ask other teachers if you can present the plays to their classes.** Invite parents, too. They will enjoy seeing their children perform. Have fun!

Chapter Ten

CAN A LITTLE MOUSE HELP A BIG MAN?

Based on an African Folktale

Characters: Narrator Man Mouse Lion

Narrator: One day a hunter went with his dog to hunt for food for his family. On the way, he met a little mouse.

Mouse: I am hurt. I cannot get to my home. Please help me. If I do not get to my home, I will die.

Hunter: I will help you.

Narrator: The hunter picked up the little mouse and helped him to his home.

Mouse: Thank you. Someday I will help you, too.

Hunter: Ha. Ha. Ha. How can a little mouse help a big man?

Narrator: A few weeks later, the hunter and his dog went hunting again. It began to rain very hard. They ran into a cave so they would not get wet. A lion was in the cave.

Lion: Good. You are just in time for lunch. You will eat your dog. Then I will eat you. That way we will both have lunch.

Narrator: The lion laughed a huge roaring laugh. Just then a loud voice came from the back of the cave.

Mouse: (in a deep voice) Good. The man will eat his dog. You will eat the hunter. Then I will eat you. That way we will all three have lunch.

Narrator: The lion could not see who was talking. He ran from the cave.

The little mouse came from the back of the cave.

Mouse: Now you see how a little mouse can help a big man.

Can a Little Mouse Help a Big Man?
Student Handout

My name is _____.

Today is _____.

Let's make words.

w<u>ent</u>	b ___ ___ ___	d ___ ___ ___	l ___ ___ ___
	t ___ ___ ___	s ___ ___ ___	
c<u>ave</u>	g ___ ___ ___	r ___ ___ ___	s ___ ___ ___
m<u>ouse</u>	bl ___ ___ ___ ___	h ___ ___ ___ ___	
h<u>ow</u>	b ___ ___ c ___ ___ ___	n ___ ___ ___ pl ___ ___	w ___ ___
l<u>unch</u>	b ___ ___ ___ ___	cr ___ ___ ___ ___	
	h ___ ___ ___ ___	m ___ ___ ___ ___	

Find these words: went   cave   mouse   how   lunch

```
m w e n t d s a t l u n c h k
c a v e n p r s h h o w c s d
i n f u p d o g a s m o u s e
```

Did you find any other words? _____

How do the man's feelings about the little mouse change in the story?

_____

_____

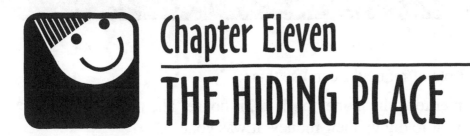

Chapter Eleven

THE HIDING PLACE

Based on a Jewish Folktale

Characters: Narrator Husband Wife Farmer

Narrator: Once a man and his wife were far from their home. They had a lot of money with them. They wanted to rest for the night, but they were afraid someone would take the money.

Man: What can we do to keep the money safe?

Wife: We must find a place to hide it.

Narrator: The man and his wife looked for a good place to hide their money. They walked and walked until they came to a big field.

Man: Maybe we can hide the money somewhere in this field.

Wife: There is a big tree over there. We can dig a hole and put the money there. We can come and get it tomorrow after we have rested.

Narrator: The man and his wife dug a hole under the big tree. They put the money in the hole. Then they covered it with dirt. They did not see the farmer at the side of the field watching them.

Man: There. No one will find our money there. It is safe.

Wife: Yes, it is safe here. We will come back tomorrow to get it and be on our way.

Narrator: The man and his wife went to the inn for a good night's rest. The farmer who owned the field walked over to the tree.

Farmer: What did the man and woman put here? Maybe it is something I can use.

Narrator: The farmer dug up the money. He was very happy.

Farmer: Money! Lots of money! I can use this.

Narrator: The farmer took the money back to his house. The next day, the man and his wife went to dig up their money. It was gone.

Man: Where is our money?

Wife: Someone has taken it. But who could it be?

Man: It must be the farmer who owns this field. We must find him.

Wife: What good will it do to find the farmer?

Man: I have a plan. We will get our money back.

Narrator: The man and his wife went to the farmer who owned the field.

Man: My wife and I are far from our home. We have a lot of money. I buried some of it in your field. If it is a safe place to hide money, I will hide more money there.

Farmer: My field is a safe place for your money. You can hide all your money there.

Man: We will be back tonight. If I find my money still in your field, I will put all my money there.

Narrator: The owner of the field ran and put the money he had taken back in the hole.

Farmer: If that man finds his money safe here, he will put more in the hole. Then I can take all the money. I will be a very rich man.

Narrator: The man and his wife went back to the field that night. They found their money in the hole where they had put it.

Wife: Come, husband, let us take our money and go before the farmer sees us.

Man: Yes, we must be on our way. The farmer will not be happy when he sees how we have tricked him.

Wife: You are a very wise man, husband. You are a very wise and tricky man.

The Hiding Place
Student Handout

My name is _____.

Today is _____.

Let's make words.

<u>f</u>ar   b __ __   c __ __   j __ __   t __ __

<u>r</u>est   b __ __ __   n __ __ __   p __ __ __   t __ __ __

<u>n</u>ight   f __ __ __ __   l __ __ __ __   m __ __ __ __

<u>hi</u>de   r __ __ __   s __ __ __   t __ __ __   w __ __ __

Fill in a word from above.

I go to bed at _____.

We play a game where someone can _____.

My little brother is a _____.

Mom takes us to school in the _____.

How did the man trick the farmer who owned the field?

_____

_____

_____.

How did the farmer feel when he didn't find any money?

_____

_____.

Chapter Twelve
THE COST OF A SMELL

Based on a French Folktale

Characters: Narrator   Baker (boy or girl)   Man   Judge (boy or girl)

Narrator: Once there was a baker who made the best pies in all the world. The pies tasted good, and they smelled good, too.

Baker: Look at all these good pies I have made. I will put them on the windowsill to cool. Soon I will sell all my pies, and I will be very rich.

Narrator: The smell of the pies went out over the land. Many people came to buy the baker's pies. When there were only two pies left, a poor man came to the baker's shop.

Man: Your pies look so good. Will you give me some pie?

Baker: No, I will not give you any pie. If you want pie, you will have to buy one.

Man: I have no money. But I will stand here and smell your pies. The smell is so good that it will fill me up.

Narrator: The man smelled and smelled the pies until he was not hungry anymore.

Man: Your pies are so good that the smell alone has filled my belly. I am not hungry anymore. Thank you.

Baker: I need more than thanks. Since the smell of my pies has filled your belly, you will have to pay me.

Man: Pay you for smelling your pies? You are very silly.

Baker: We will see how silly I am. I will call the judge.

Narrator: The baker called the judge, who came right away.

Judge: What is going on here? Why have you called me?

Baker: This man has smelled all my pies, and the smell has filled him up. Now he will not pay me for his filling his belly.

Judge: So that is your story. Let me hear this man's story, too.

Man: I was hungry, but I had no money to buy a pie. So I smelled and smelled until my belly was full.

Narrator: The judge looked at the baker. He looked at the man. He spoke to the man.

Judge: You have filled your belly with the smell of this baker's pies. It is only right that you pay.

Man: But I have no money.

Judge: Don't worry about that.

Narrator: The judge took two gold coins from his pocket. He gave them to the man and told the baker to open up his (her) hands. Then he spoke to the man.

Judge: Hit these coins together as hard as you can.

Narrator: The man hit the coins as hard as he could. Ping, ping, ping went the coins.

Judge: Do it again. Hit them harder.

Narrator: The man hit the coins together. Clang, clang, clang went the coins. Then the judge turned to the baker.

Judge: Baker, you have filled this man's belly with a smell. Now he has filled your hands with a sound. We will talk of this matter no more.

Narrator: The judge gave a great big laugh. The poor man gave a great big laugh. And the silly baker never tried to make anyone pay for smelling pies again.

The Cost of a Smell Student Handout

My name is _____.

Today is _____.

Let's make words.

smell   b_ _ _   f_ _ _   s _ _ _ _   t_ _ _ _   w_ _ _

bake   c_ _ _ _   f_ _ _ _   l_ _ _ _   m_ _ _ _

           r_ _ _ _   t_ _ _ _   w_ _ _ _

judge   b_ _ _ _ _   f_ _ _ _ _

sound   b_ _ _ _ _   f_ _ _ _ _   h_ _ _ _ _

           m_ _ _ _ _   p_ _ _ _ _   r_ _ _ _ _

Let's use our words.

I can _____ a pie.   tell   well   smell

I _____ a little dog.   pound   found   sound

Can you _____ a cake?   rake   bake   lake

What kind of a person was the baker?

_____

_____

_____

_____

Chapter Thirteen
THE FOUR GOOD FRIENDS

Vocabulary practice: donkey   rooster   city   master   mistress   robbers

Characters: First Narrator   Second Narrator   Cat   Donkey   Dog
Rooster   First Robber   Second Robber

First Narrator: Once there were a dog, a cat, a donkey, and a rooster who were good friends.

Dog: I want to run away from my master. He wants me to hunt, but I am too old and tired. I want to rest and chew on good bones.

Cat: I want to run away, too. I like to lie by the fire and sleep, but my mistress wants me to chase mice.

Rooster: If you run away, I will go with you. My master says I am too loud in the morning. I like to crow as loud as I can.

Donkey: I may as well go, too. There is not very much hay on this farm for me to eat.

Dog: Why don't we go to the big city and become singers?

Donkey: Yes, I am a very good singer.

Rooster: I am always singing. I can sing very loud.

Cat: We must try singing together before we start out.

Second Narrator: So the animals practiced their singing all together.

Dog: Woof, woof, woof, woof.

Cat: Meow, meow, meow, meow.

Rooster: Cock-a-doodle-doo. Cock-a-doodle-doo.

Donkey: Hee-haw. Hee-haw. Hee-haw.

Dog: What beautiful music we make together. Everyone will love our singing in the big city. Come on, let's get going. The city is far away.

First Narrator: The four animals walked and walked. When they came to a forest, they rested. They were all very tired.

Second Narrator: After they slept a little while, the Rooster woke them up.

Rooster: Cock-a-doodle-doo. Cock-a-doodle-doo.

Dog: Be quiet. It's not morning yet. It is still night.

Rooster: I see a light in the trees. It is not the sun. Maybe it is someone who can give us food and a place to stay.

Cat: I would love a nice fire to warm me.

Donkey: I would like some good fresh hay to eat.

Dog: Yes. A big bone to chew on would be good.

Rooster: And maybe there is a high roof where I can sleep until it is time for me to wake everyone up in the morning.

Dog: Let's go. Maybe we will find some new friends.

First Narrator: The four singers followed the light to a small blue house at the edge of the woods. The rooster sat on a windowsill and looked into the house.

Dog: What do you see?

Rooster: I see a lot of food, and I see two men sitting at a table eating it all up.

Second Narrator: The four friends did not know that the two men in the house were robbers.

Cat: Maybe if we sing for them, they will share their food and home with us.

Dog: That is a good idea.

First Narrator: So the dog climbed on the donkey's back, the cat climbed on the dog's back, and the rooster sat on top of the cat. They stood at the window and sang.

Dog: Woof, woof, woof, woof.

Cat: Meow, meow, meow, meow.

Rooster: Cock-a-doodle-doo. Cock-a-doodle-doo.

Donkey: Hee-haw. Hee-haw. Hee-haw.

Second Narrator: The animals sang so loud and hard that the rooster, cat, and dog fell through the window. The donkey jumped in after them. The robbers were frightened, and they ran off into the forest.

First Narrator: The four friends ate and ate and ate the robbers' food until they were too full to move. They wanted to sleep.

Dog: I will take my bone with me and sleep by the door.

Cat: I will lie down by the fire. That is my favorite place to sleep.

Donkey: I will sleep outside. If I wake up I can eat some sweet hay.

Rooster: There is a nice high roof for me. I will be ready to sing early in the morning.

First Narrator: The animals were soon fast asleep. They did not know it, but the two robbers were watching the house.

First Robber: When it is dark, I will go back to our house to see what kind of monster scared us.

Second Narrator: When the lights went out, the robber crept back into the house to see what he could see. He went into the kitchen. The cat woke and opened her eyes. The robber thought the cat's eyes were sparks from the fire. He tried to kick them back into the fireplace. That did not make the cat very happy.

Cat: Yeow! Hiss! Meow!

First Narrator: The cat jumped on the robber and scratched him. Then she picked up some hot coals with the coal shovel and threw them on the robber.

First Robber: Ow! Ow! Help!

Second Narrator: The robber tried to run out the kitchen door, but he fell over the dog, and banged his knee on the dog's big bone.

Dog: Woof, woof! Growl.

First Narrator: The dog picked up the bone in his teeth, and hit the robber with it so hard he knocked him out the door.

First Robber: Ow! Ow! Help!

Second Narrator: The robber ran right into the donkey, who kicked him so hard he fell in a big pile of hay. The hay got in his mouth and in his nose and in his ears.

Donkey: Hee-haw. Hee-haw. Hee-haw.

First Robber: Ow! Ow! Help!

First Narrator: The robber jumped up and screamed so loud he woke the rooster, who thought it was morning. The rooster flew round and round the robber's head flapping his wings and crowing.

Rooster: Cock-a-doodle-doo! Cock-a-doodle-doo! Cock-a-doodle-doo!

First Narrator: The robber ran to his friend in the forest as fast as he could.

First Robber: A dragon was by the fire. She scratched me and breathed fire on me. A policeman was by the door. He beat me with his club. A huge monster in the yard threw me as high as the moon and put scratchy sticks in my eyes and my ears and my nose. And a million bats flew around my head, screaming at me.

Second Robber: I am not afraid of a dragon. I am not afraid of a monster. And I am not afraid of bats. But maybe the policeman is after us. He might put us in jail. We'd better run as far from that house as we can.

Second Narrator: The robbers ran far, far away from the house in the woods, and they never came back.

First Narrator: The four singers enjoyed their new home so much that they never went to the big city. Someday you may be in a forest, and you may hear this song.

Dog: Woof, woof, woof, woof.

Cat: Meow, meow, meow, meow.

Rooster: Cock-a-doodle-doo. Cock-a-doodle-doo.

Donkey: Hee-haw. Hee-haw. Hee-haw.

First and Second Narrators: If you do, you will know you are near the house of the four good friends.

The Four Good Friends
Student Handout

My name is _____.

Today is _____.

Let's make words.

leftover = left + over   doghouse = dog + house   someone = some + one

rooftop =   _____+_____

into =   _____+_____

something =   _____+_____

doorway =   _____+_____

fireplace =   _____+_____

Let's use our words.

The four friends went _____ the woods.

They wanted _____ to eat.

The cat slept by the _____.

The dog lay by the _____.

The rooster flew to the _____.

Do you think the four friends are sorry they did not get to the big city?

_____

_____

_____

_____

Chapter Fourteen
MORE FUN WITH ROLE-PLAY

Reading and performing in plays is usually enjoyable to young children and an excellent way to provide reading practice. Not only do the children have to read the words correctly, they must show they comprehend what they are reading by the way they express themselves.

After you have performed all the plays in this book, think about adding other role-playing activities. Acting out and providing dialogue to familiar stories is good practice in recalling sequences of events. Start with well known fairy tales, such as *The Three Bears* or *The Three Pigs*. Read one to the students, and then ask for volunteers to act out the story using whatever words they remember in the appropriate places. Choose children to portray all the characters except the narrator, which should be played by the teacher or another adult.

Here's how *The Three Bears* might go:

Narrator: Once there were three bears, Mama Bear, Papa Bear, and Baby Bear. One morning they sat down to eat their porridge.
Papa Bear: My porridge is too hot.
Mama Bear: My porridge is too hot.
Baby Bear: My porridge is too hot, too.
Mama Bear: Let's go for a walk.
Narrator: The three bears went for a walk. While they were gone, a little girl named Goldilocks came to their house. She was hungry. She tasted the porridge in all the bowls.

Goldilocks: This porridge is too hot. This porridge is too cold. This porridge is just right.

Narrator: And Goldilocks ate all of Baby Bear's porridge. Then she decided to sit down.

Goldilocks: This chair is too big. This chair is too small. This chair is just right.

Narrator: Goldilocks sat down in Baby Bear's chair and it broke into pieces. Then Goldilocks decided to take a nap.

Goldilocks: This bed is too hard. This bed is too soft. This bed is just right.

Narrator: Goldilocks lay down in Baby Bear's bed and fell fast asleep. Just then the three bears came back from their walk.

Papa Bear: Someone's been eating my porridge.

Mama Bear: Someone's been eating my porridge.

Baby Bear: Someone's been eating my porridge and it's all gone.

Papa Bear: Someone's been sitting in my chair.

Mama Bear: Someone's been sitting in my chair.

Baby Bear: Someone's been sitting in my chair and it's all broken.

Papa Bear: Someone's been sleeping in my bed.

Mama Bear: Someone's been sleeping in my bed.

Baby Bear: Someone's been sleeping in my bed and she's still here.

Narrator: Goldilocks woke up, and she jumped out the window. The three bears never saw her again.

After the children have performed several plays this way, try writing your own plays from favorite stories. This activity provides practice in recognizing the main parts of a story and selecting appropriate dialogue to convey the story line in proper sequence.

Read a short story that the children enjoy, and say that you will be using this story to write a play. Ask the children to tell you the most important parts of the story, and list them on the board. Make a list of characters, including a narrator or two. Have the children recall the sequence of events and devise dialogue for the characters by asking how the narrator might introduce the story and what each character would say. After the class agrees that the suggested words are appropriate, write down what they dictate to you.

Let's use a short fable to demonstrate how the process works:

The Tortoise and the Hare

Important
events:

The hare challenges the tortoise to a race.

The tortoise agrees to race.

The race starts; the hare thinks he will win.

The hare goes to sleep.

The tortoise passes the hare while he is sleeping.

The tortoise wins the race.

Characters: Narrator

Hare

Tortoise

Narrator: Once there was a tortoise and a hare.

Hare: I think I will dare Tortoise to race me. Then I can show everybody how fast I am. Hey, Tortoise, do you want to race me?

Tortoise: Yes, I will race you.

Hare: Well, let's go. Ready, set, go.

Narrator: The hare took off going very fast, while the tortoise took one slow step after another.

Tortoise: I may not be as fast as the hare, but I will do my best to win the race.

Hare: That tortoise is so slow. I think I will rest for a little while. I can still win the race.

Narrator: The hare sat under a tree and fell fast asleep. The tortoise kept going, slow and steady.

Tortoise: Oh, look. There is the hare sleeping under the tree. I will go by him very quietly, and I will win the race.

Narrator: The tortoise went by the hare and just as he was crossing the finish line, the hare woke up and saw that he had lost the race.

Hare: Oh, no. How could I lose a race to a tortoise?

Narrator: The hare never asked the tortoise to race again.

After you have written the play, type it up, distribute it to the children, and act it out as many times as they wish. In this one activity, you have practiced many skills: sequencing, outlining (choosing the main events), writing, choosing the best words, speaking, and reading.

In addition, hopefully your children have gained, from all their role-playing experiences, self-confidence in their ability to speak before a group, a skill that will benefit them throughout their entire lives.

Printed in the USA
CPSIA information can be obtained
at www.ICGtesting.com
LVHW080723170724
785510LV00007B/275